HOLT
1
FRENCH

Reading Strategies and Skills Handbook

For use with French 1, *Allez, viens!* and *Joie de lire*

HOLT, RINEHART AND WINSTON

A Harcourt Classroom Education Company

Austin · New York · Orlando · Atlanta · San Francisco · Boston · Dallas · Toronto · London

This book was adapted from the *Reading Strategies Handbook for High School: A Guide to Teaching Reading in the Literature Classroom* by Dr. Kylene Beers. Our special thanks to her for allowing us to share with foreign language teachers her experiences and the powerful insights she gained in her "journey to understanding" of the problems and challenges faced by struggling readers.

Table of Contents

Strategies

Strategies Applied to Readings in *Allez, viens!*

To the Teacher

This handbook of strategies came about because Dr. Kylene Beers, through a series of personal encounters in her literature classes with the problems and challenges of struggling readers, came to understand a very basic truth. For students who know how to do such skills as generalizing, analyzing, making connections, making predictions, seeing causal relationships, keeping events in sequence, and so forth, worksheets that call for them to practice those skills are simply that: practice. The worksheets offer these students no new insights; even worse, for students who can't do these things in the first place, skills worksheets are just another opportunity for failing. For neither group are they a vehicle for learning.

Once the realization is accepted that some students do not know how to perform the skills that we sometimes assume in a class where reading is supposed to be taking place, the next step is to figure out how to get from point A (the student can't do the skill and may not even understand the underlying concept) to point B (the student is able to do the skill).

At the Intersection of Skills and Strategies

Most students can do the higher order thinking skills; they just don't know that they are doing them, and they certainly don't know how to connect the skills to something they are reading. Students analyze music, make comparisons about fashion, and make inferences about their friends' behavior on a daily basis. They just need to be guided to apply these thinking skills to something they are reading, for reading skills are really no more than thinking skills applied to a reading situation. To make the leap of applying thinking skills they already know to a reading selection, students need strategies—something to serve as a scaffold or framework for the thinking skills they are learning to apply; a vehicle for getting to the thinking skills they already possess but haven't figured out how to use in a reading context.

Reading strategies can create a learning environment that encourages certain types of thinking. Because reading strategies promote many different kinds of thinking, they are inherently flexible and adaptable. Multiple strategies can be used to help students master the same skills, thus addressing the diverse needs and learning styles of today's student population. In the same way, each strategy can be used to teach a multitude of reading skills.

Strategies and Students: Who Benefits?

Strategies help all learners, not just struggling ones. Skilled readers are skilled, in part, because they understand how to make sense of texts. They know how to apply all those things we call reading skills without having to work through the process of a strategy. But less-skilled readers need the scaffold a strategy provides.

Less-skilled readers often think that skilled readers simply open a book, let their eyes fly over words, and then understand all there is to understand. Struggling readers don't see all the cognitive processes that skilled readers use to make meaning. They don't see the rereading, the inferencing, the generalizing, the connecting, the comparing, the predicting, the sequencing. They just see that certain students always seem to know the right answers; they don't realize that so much thinking goes on with reading.

The strategies in this book work just as effectively with gifted students who are excellent readers as they do with struggling readers. It's just a matter of deciding which strategy works best with each type of student. When trying to decide which strategy to use with a particular student, always ask yourself how the strategy benefits the student. If the only benefit is that the student gets practice with a skill he or she already possesses, then use another strategy.

Strategies and Assessment: An Important Connection

When you're using strategies, there are three types of assessments to consider.

- First, you should assess whether or not the strategy is resulting in the types of reading skills (thinking skills) the student needs.

- Second—though this is not applicable to all strategies—you should assess the quality of the product that results from some strategies. (For instance, Text Reformulation results in a written product.)

- Third, you should provide students with the opportunity to assess their own use of a particular strategy.

To assess whether a strategy is yielding the type of thinking the student needs, you have to listen attentively to students' comments. If you aren't doing that, you aren't hearing evidence of the thinking that strategies encourage. If you don't hear evidence of their thinking, then you really don't know if the strategy is effective or not, especially the strategies that don't result in a written product. As students use the strategies, try to capture their comments on paper and then look at those comments to see what insights they offer you into your students' thinking. That glimpse into their thinking processes will give you valuable information that can point the way to the direction you will take your teaching next.

In addition to assessing students' thinking, some of the strategies (Somebody Wanted But So, Text Reformulation, Story Impressions, and Save the Last Word for Me) result in specific written products. These written products can be assessed in the same way you would any piece of writing your students create.

Finally, it is important to let students participate in self-assessment. To help students see how strategies are benefiting them, have them occasionally complete a brief survey like the one below.

Name _____ Date _____

Strategy _____

Complete each statement:

1. I like this strategy because ... _____

_____

2. I dislike this strategy because ... _____

_____

3. This strategy helps me... _____

_____

For almost every strategy, there is something specific you can do to add to the general assessment. Again, the point is to help students see that reading involves thinking and that strategies encourage them to engage in the kind of thinking they need to be doing.

This book is divided into two parts. The first part of the book is devoted to the strategies themselves: a definition of each one, how they can best be applied to a text, and the skills that they target. In this first section of the book, you will find the following information:

- In the Table of Contents there is a brief definition of each strategy, as well as a list of which strategies will be applied in the chapters of *Allez, viens!* Level 1.

- On pages ix-x, you will find a table that shows how each strategy can best be applied to any kind of reading.

- The tables on pages xi – xiv give you information about applying the strategies to readings in the **Lisons!** section of the *Pupil's Edition* and reading selections in *Joie de lire*, the French 1 reader.

- Following these tables, on pp. xv-xvii, there is a list of the skills that can be targeted with these strategies.

- The chart on page xviii gives examples of the kinds of comments students might make when they use the reading strategies, and a form that can be used to track the use of the strategies by listening to and recording student expressions.

In the second part of this *Reading Strategies and Skills Handbook*, you will find activity masters that are connected to the readings in the **Lisons!** section of each chapter of the *Pupil's Edition*. You can use these activity masters to apply the strategies to the reading texts in order to target specific skills. When you want to apply one of the strategies to a reading selection in *Joie de lire*, you should use one of the activity masters in the first part of the handbook.

		STRATEGIES AND SKILLS: How They Can Best Be Used		
Reading Strategy	**Reading Skill**	**When can I use this strategy?**		
		Before Reading	**During Reading**	**After Reading**
Anticipation Guide	Making Predictions	✓		
	Using Prior Knowledge	✓		
	Analyzing Cause and Effect Relationships		✓	
	Analyzing Persuasive Techniques			✓
	Making Generalizations			✓
It Says ... I Say	Making Inferences		✓	
	Making Generalizations			✓
	Drawing Conclusions			✓
Logographic Cues	Understanding Text Structure	✓		✓
	Making Generalizations			✓
Most Important Word	Identifying the Main Idea			✓
	Making Generalizations			✓
	Summarizing			✓
Probable Passage	Making Predictions	✓		
	Identifying Purpose	✓		✓
	Comparing and Contrasting			✓
	Analyzing Chronological Order			✓
Read, Rate, Reread	Making Inferences		✓	
	Determining the Writer's Purpose			✓
	Identifying the Main Idea			✓
Retellings	Analyzing Chronological Order			✓
	Identifying the Main Idea			✓
	Summarizing			✓

STRATEGIES AND SKILLS: How They Can Best Be Used

Reading Strategy	Reading Skill	When can I use this strategy?		
		Before Reading	During Reading	After Reading
Save the Last Word for Me	Comparing and Contrasting			✓
	Determining the Main Idea			✓
Say Something	Monitoring Reading		✓	
	Using Prior Knowledge	✓		
Sketch to Stretch	Drawing on Your Own Experience	✓		
	Drawing Conclusions			✓
	Making Generalizations			✓
	Analyzing Cause and Effect			✓
	Summarizing			✓
Somebody Wanted But So	Analyzing Cause and Effect			✓
	Summarizing			✓
Story Impressions	Making Predictions	✓		
	Analyzing Cause and Effect		✓	
	Making Inferences		✓	
	Analyzing Chronological Order			✓
	Identifying Purpose			✓
	Comparing and Contrasting			✓
Tea Party	Making Predictions	✓		
	Using Prior Knowledge	✓		
Text Reformulation	Understanding Text Structure			✓
	Analyzing Cause and Effect			✓
Think Aloud	Monitoring Reading		✓	

APPLYING READING STRATEGIES AND SKILLS
to French 1 *Allez, viens!* and *Joie de lire*

	Allez, viens! Pupil's Edition (reading selections in **Lisons!**)	*Reading Strategies and Skills Handbook* (prepared Activity Master for *Pupil's Edition* reading)	*Joie de lire* Level 1 reader	*Reading Strategies and Skills Handbook* (suggested strategy and Activity Master template)
Chapitre 1	**Petites Annonces** (pen-pal ads by French teenagers) pp. 36-37	Anticipation Guide (making generalizations **Activity Master, p. 65** Say Something (connecting reading to personal experience) **Activity Master, p. 66**	**Le Club des quatre** (narrative; story of four young people who live in Montfort, France) **Les Correspondantes** (letters between two pen-pals)	Think Aloud (monitoring comprehension) **Activity Master, p. 61** It Says ... I Say (comparing aand contrasting) **Activity Master, p. 9**
Chapitre 2	**Sondage : Les lycéens ont-ils le moral?** (Survey: French students' attitudes toward school) pp. 64-65	Read, Rate, Reread (identifying the main idea) **Activity Master, p. 67** Think Aloud (monitoring comprehension) **Activity Master, p. 68**	**La Disparition d'Olivier** (continuing story of the four young people) **C'est bientôt l'heure des Mamans** (a poem)	Say Something (monitoring reading) **Activity Master, p. 37** Most Important Word (identifying the main idea) **Activity Master, p. 17**
Chapitre 3	**Univers: Tout pour la rentrée** (ads for school supplies) pp. 92-93	Say Something (monitoring comprehension) **Activity Master, p. 69** Read, Rate, Reread (making inferences) **Activity Master, p. 70**	**L'Enquête du club des quatre** (narrative text; continuing story of the four young people) **J'ai vu...** (a poem)	Anticipation Guide (making predictions) **Activity Master, p. 5** Logographic Cues (understanding text structure) **Activity Master, p. 13**

APPLYING READING STRATEGIES AND SKILLS
to French 1 *Allez, viens!* and *Joie de lire*

	Allez, viens! Pupil's Edition (reading selections in **Lisons!**)	*Reading Strategies and Skills Handbook* (prepared Activity Master for *Pupil's Edition* reading)	*Joie de lire* Level 1 reader	*Reading Strategies and Skills Handbook* (suggested strategy and Activity Master template)
Chapitre 4	Allez, c'est à vous de choisir! (short articles about activities and hobbies) pp. 126-127	Tea Party (making predictions) **Activity Masters, pp. 71, 72** Think Aloud (monitoring comprehension) **Activity Master, p. 73**	Le Club des quatre à la Maison des jeunes (narrative; activities at the youth center) Le Sport au Québec (narrative; description of some Canadian sports)	Retellings (summarizing) Activity Master, pp. 28–29 Think Aloud (monitoring reading) Activity Master, p. 62
Chapitre 5	Des menus de cafés (French menus) pp. 158-159	Read, Rate, Reread (making inferences) **Activity Master, p. 74** Say Something (monitoring comprehension) **Activity Master, p. 75**	Les Cafés parisiens (Description of two cafés in Paris) Les Croissants (a cartoon)	Anticipation Guide (making generalizations) **Activity Master, p. 5** Retellings (identifying the main idea) **Activity Master, pp. 28–29**
Chapitre 6	Parcs d'attractions (Theme park ads) pp. 188-189	Think Aloud (monitoring comprehension) **Activity Master, p. 77** Tea Party (making predictions) **Activity Masters, pp. 78, 79**	Un jeune Américain à Paris (narrative. Two young people meet at the Louvre museum - go to a café and theater) Le Cinéma : les jeunes l'aiment	Story Impressions (making predictions) **Activity Master, p. 49** Most Important Word (identifying the main idea) **Activity Master, p. 17**

APPLYING READING STRATEGIES AND SKILLS
to French 1 *Allez, viens!* and *Joie de lire*

	Allez, viens! **Pupil's Edition** (reading selections in **Lisons!**)	*Reading Strategies and Skills Handbook* (prepared Activity Master for *Pupil's Edition* reading)	*Joie de lire* Level 1 reader	*Reading Strategies and Skills Handbook* (suggested strategy and Activity Master template)
Chapitre 7	En direct des refuges (French pet adoption ads) pp. 216-217	Text Reformulation (understanding text structure) **Activity Master, p. 80** Logographic Cues (understanding text structure) **Activity Master, p. 81**	La Cantatrice chauve (Play by Ionesco) Histoires drôles (Jokes)	Read, Rate, Reread (determining the writer's purpose) **Activity Master, p. 25** Sketch to Stretch (analyzing cause and effect) **Activity Master, p. 41**
Chapitre 8	La cuisine africaine (recipes for African dishes) pp. 250-251	Tea Party (making predictions) **Activity Masters, pp. 82, 83** Read, Rate, Reread (monitoring comprehension) **Activity Master, p. 84**	Au supermarché pour la première fois (narrative) La Cantine (narrative)	Story Impressions (making a prediction) **Activity Master, p. 49** Save the Last Word for Me (comparing and contrasting) **Activity Master, p. 33**
Chapitre 9	Je passe ma vie au téléphone (article about the telephone habits of some francophone teenagers) pp. 282-283	Read, Rate, Reread (making inferences) **Activity Master, p. 85** Save the Last Word for Me (determining the main idea) **Activity Master, p. 86**	La Tentation (narrative)	Story Impressions (making predictions) **Activity Master, p. 49** Anticipation Guide (making generalizations) **Activity Master, p. 5**

APPLYING READING STRATEGIES AND SKILLS
to French 1 *Allez, viens!* and *Joie de lire*

	Allez, viens! **Pupil's Edition** (reading selections in **Lisons!**)	*Reading Strategies and Skills Handbook* (prepared Activity Master for *Pupil's Edition* reading)	*Joie de lire* Level 1 reader	*Reading Strategies and Skills Handbook* (suggested strategy and Activity Master template)
Chapitre 10	La mode au lycée (article about teenagers' attitudes toward fashion) pp. 312-313	It Says … I Say (making inferences) **Activity Master, p. 87** Most Important Word (determining the main idea) **Activity Master, p. 88**	Les Habits neufs de l'empereur (Narrative from a fairy tale of Andersen) Maeva, la nouvelle génération mode (narrative)	Tea Party (using prior knowledge) **Activity Master, pp. 52–53** Save the Last Word for Me (comparing and contrasting) **Activity Master, p. 33**
Chapitre 11	Un guide touristique (tourist information for Provence) pp. 340-341	Say Something (monitoring comprehension) **Activity Master, p. 89** Think Aloud (monitoring comprehension) **Activity Master, p. 90**	Olivier fait de la voile (narrative- continuing story of four young people)	Tea Party (making predictions) **Activity Master, pp. 52–53** Text Reformulation (understanding text structure) **Activity Master, p. 57**
Chapitre 12	Cheval de bois (A Creole story from Martinique) pp. 374-375	Story Impressions (making predictions) **Activity Master, p. 91** Probable Passage (making predictions) **Activity Master, p. 92**	Compère Chien et Compère Chat (narrative - Créole tale)	Say Something (monitoring reading) **Activity Master, p. 37** Somebody Wanted But So (summarizing) **Activity Master, p. 45**

Summary of Skills Targeted

Analyzing Cause and Effect

A **cause** makes something happen. An **effect** is what happens as a result of that cause. If a writer states the cause and not the effect, or states the effect and not the cause, the reader must make inferences in order to determine the probable cause or the probable effect. To analyze cause-and-effect relationships, we must use information in the text along with our own prior knowledge and experience of how things happen.

Analyzing Chronological Order

Chronological order is the sequence in which events happen. As readers, we identify and understand the order of events in a text by analyzing the text's structure. Analyzing the chronological order of a text reveals the ways in which writers organize and present ideas, as well as the purpose of a text.

Analyzing Persuasion

Persuasive techniques are devices that a writer uses to convince a reader to take action or to believe or think a certain way about a subject, idea, event, or person. In persuasive writing, writers use logical appeals (reasons, facts, statistics, and examples) or emotional appeals (words, phrases, and anecdotes that appeal strongly to the reader's feelings, fears, hopes, and beliefs) or a combination of both techniques.

Comparing and Contrasting

(includes the skills **recognizing comparison and contrast, comparing texts**)
Comparing means "seeing similarities." **Contrasting** means "seeing differences." As readers, we often make comparisons and contrasts among texts and various characters, as well as between a text and our own experiences, ideas, and opinions. Analyzing similarities and differences both within and across texts is an important skill to cultivate. This skill in turn develops the ability to draw conclusions, make inferences, and determine cause and effect, as well as to promote general comprehension.

Connecting Literature to Current Events

Just as journalists write about real-life events for news articles, fiction writers also often base what they write on actual events. As active readers, we draw on our experience and knowledge of current events to inform our understanding of the texts we read. In the process, we draw parallels between the world inside a text and the world in which we live. **Connecting literature to current events** is one way that we find significance and relevance in what we read.

Determining the Main Idea

Recognizing the overall meaning of a text helps us as readers to understand what we read. The **main idea** is the most important idea that the writer wants readers to remember about the topic—the message, opinion, insight, or lesson that is the focus or key idea of the text. The supporting details (such as facts and ideas) are the bits of information that the writer includes to further develop, explain, or illustrate the main idea. Sometimes the main idea is directly stated; at other times, it is implied within the text. Often we must "read between the lines," or infer meaning from what is read, looking closely at the important details while thinking about the meaning of those details. From this inference, we can then identify the main idea for ourselves.

Determining Main Idea and Relevant Details

As readers, we determine the main idea and identify relevant details, methods of development, and their effectiveness in a variety of types of written material.

Determining Writer's Purpose, also called Recognizing Author's Purpose

Skilled readers recognize the ways a writer can influence their thinking. One way readers do this is by **determining the writer's purpose.** The writer's purpose may be to explain or inform; to create a mood or stir an emotion; to tell a story or narrate a series of events; or to persuade the reader to believe something or do something. A writer's purpose often influences a reader's purpose. Whether the writer's intention is to inform, persuade, or describe, readers react not only to the words, but also to the writer's purpose. Determining the writer's purpose helps readers to approach, respond to, appreciate, and evaluate a text more appropriately.

Distinguishing Fact from Opinion

Distinguishing between statements of **fact** and statements of **opinion** helps readers judge the validity of a writer's viewpoint and understand a writer's motivation. As readers, we must learn to understand the writer's perspective: the viewpoint

Reading Strategies and Skills Handbook **XV**

from which the writer presents his or her material. Part of this task involves recognizing the difference between a statement of fact and a statement of opinion, because writers sometimes state an opinion as fact.

Strategic readers also **form opinions** and revise them as they read. Opinions can be influenced by specific details in the text, the reader's prior knowledge and experience, and discussions the reader has with other readers. Opinions can be supported with details from the text or from the reader's own experience.

Drawing/Making Inferences

As readers, we make **inferences** when we combine information in the text with what we already know in order to understand things the writer has not stated directly in the text. When we use information in the text and information we already know to make an inference that is specific to the text, we are **drawing a conclusion.** When we use information in the text and information we already know to make an inference that extends beyond a specific text to the general world, we are making a generalization.

Evaluating Motivation and Credibility

Readers evaluate a writer's **motivation** by thinking about why the writer wanted to write about a particular topic. To evaluate the **credibility** of a text, readers judge how believable they think the text is. Are the arguments convincing? Can they be proven? Readers determine whether the facts of the text can be verified and consider how the writer's motivation might have affected the credibility of the text.

Evaluating Written Information

A student locates, gathers, analyzes, and evaluates written information for a variety of purposes, including research projects, real-world tasks, and self-improvement.

Identifying Purpose

(includes the skills **establishing and adjusting purposes for reading, setting purposes for reading, identifying a text's purpose**)

A reader's purpose for reading is his or her motive for reading a text. We may read to be informed, to solve problems, to discover, to interpret, or to be entertained. **Identifying a purpose** helps us understand a text more completely and better appreciate what we are reading. Identifying a purpose also helps us to approach, respond to, and evaluate the text more appropriately. Adjusting a purpose occurs as a reader moves through the text: we make adjust-ments as necessary to changes within the text and changes in our purpose for reading.

Making a Generalization

To **make a generalization**, readers apply information from a text to the general world. As readers, we must draw some general ideas or principles from the facts and details we read in order to form a generalization.

Making generalizations is similar to drawing conclusions in that both involve examining text clues, using prior knowledge when appropriate, and inferring an explanation, cause, or rule that applies to the events in the text. However, a generalization applies to many different sets of facts, events, or situations; a conclusion is text-specific and applies to a single set of facts, events, or situations.

Making Predictions

As readers, we **make predictions** when we think about what will happen next. Our predictions are often based on inferences we make about ideas and details that writers do not reveal directly. Predictions are based on our knowledge about a topic, our general knowledge and background experience, and what is stated or implied in a text. When we make a prediction, we forecast what might happen next as a result of given actions or events, or what we think the writer is going to say.

Monitoring Comprehension

As readers, we often **monitor our comprehension** and make adjustments when necessary. When we think about what we're doing while we are reading, we can understand when we're having trouble and choose appropriate strategies to improve our comprehension of a text. Monitoring comprehension may include strategies such as rereading, asking questions, and using resources such as a dictionary or glossary.
(Monitoring comprehension may also include the skill **adjusting our reading rate.**)

Monitoring Reading

(includes the skill **Questioning**)
Monitoring reading helps us become more active readers. We monitor our reading when we think about how we are reading, recognize when we are having trouble, and choose appropriate strategies to better comprehend a text. Reading strategies are study techniques or aids that help to increase a reader's comprehension of a text. Strategies readers use to monitor their comprehension include rereading, using resources, and questioning.

Paraphrasing

A paraphrase is a type of summary in which the author's ideas are restated in the reader's own words. **Paraphrasing** is a good way for readers to check their comprehension of the original text. If they can state someone else's ideas in their own words, then they have understood what was read. Paraphrasing and summarizing are not exactly the same activity. Paraphrasing is restating or retelling in your own words. Summarizing is retelling the most important information or details of a text.

Study/Research Skills

As readers, we select and use appropriate study and research skills and tools according to the type of information being gathered or organized, including almanacs, government publications, microfiche, news sources, and information services.

Summarizing

A summary is a short restatement of the main events and essential ideas of a text. When readers summarize, they try to present a complete picture of the text using only a few words. Knowing how to summarize helps readers understand and remember what they have read. **Summarizing** helps readers share what they have read with others. Summarizing is also a useful way to record the most important point of a text, and it can help readers analyze and evaluate the material.

Using Context Clues

Our main method for developing our vocabulary is using our own knowledge and experience to decipher meanings of words or parts of words. We do this primarily through **using context clues** and recognizing prefixes, suffixes, and root words in order to determine meanings of unfamiliar words. The context of a word is the group of words or sentences surrounding it, and this context often contains clues that help readers determine the meaning of unfamiliar words. Another way to increase vocabulary is by studying and using word parts: prefixes, suffixes, and root words. Practice in adding prefixes and suffixes to words will help readers recognize those word parts in a text, thus improving the readers' vocabulary.
(This skill includes the skill **understanding regional and cultural sayings.**)

Using Prior Knowledge

As readers, we make meaning. What a text means to us depends, at least in part, on who we are. Because we have had different experiences, we see things differently. The connections we create from a text are going to be our own—drawn from our prior knowledge. **Prior knowledge** is what we already know—the information we have in our heads that helps us understand the information we read in a text. As we read, we should allow our minds to go back to our prior knowledge and experiences in order to make connections with the text. As readers, we can use strategies that allow us to search for connections between our prior knowledge and the information we are reading. These strategies can make us more active readers and aid us in comprehending and recalling a text.

As readers, we **draw on our experience** and use prior knowledge to comprehend and make connections to texts. Prior knowledge is the information we have that helps us understand what we read in a text. The meaning of a text depends, at least in part, on the knowledge we already possess. Because each reader has had different experiences, lived in different places, and known different people, he or she will see things differently. The connections we make will be our own. By using strategies that activate prior knowledge and draw on personal experience, struggling readers become more active and can better understand and remember what they read.

Using Text Organizers

Text Organizers help to present, label, categorize, and summarize information in a text in order to make it clearer and easier to understand. Text organizers include overviews, headings, summaries, and graphic features such as time lines, maps, diagrams, charts, graphs, and illustrations. Using text organizers to locate and order information in a text can help students to identify main ideas and important details.

Using Text Structures

A **text structure** is the pattern writers use to organize the ideas or events they are writing about. Writers commonly use three major patterns of organization: cause and effect, chronological order, or comparison and contrast. Although a writer may use more than one text structure, many texts have a predominant pattern, such as comparison and contrast. As readers, we first learn how to identify the predominant pattern or structure. Then we use that pattern or structure to perceive relationships, recognize outcomes, make predictions, make inferences, and draw conclusions.

Listening to Student Talk

Here are some examples of the kinds of comments you might hear students make as they engage in reading strategies. When students make the type of comment listed in the *Student Comment* column, they are demonstrating the skill listed in the *Skill* column to the left of the comment. You might want to keep this reference card handy to help you identify the specific skills students are using. You can use the back of this card to record and identify actual comments made by students.

Skill	Student Comment
Making Predictions:	"I bet the character will turn himself in at the end."
Using Chronology:	"But Rainsford hid in the tree before he set the trap for Zaroff."
Determining Cause and Effect:	"She had a miserable life because she was trying to make money to pay for the expensive necklace that she borrowed and then lost."
Determining the Main Idea:	"This is mainly about how people can be thoughtless in the way they treat people with disabilities."
Making Generalizations:	"I think this story shows that there's nothing as important as freedom."
Summarizing:	"In this story, a boy gets reward money for finding a dog he really didn't find. He winds up giving the money to the church because he feels so guilty."
Questioning the Text:	"Why did he go out into the woods and live by himself?"
Making Connections:	"I didn't like this story as much as the poem."
Making Inferences:	"Mrs. Jones seems like a person who cares about kids."
Comparing and Contrasting:	"These two characters seem a lot alike to me. Both are funny, nice, and always in trouble."
Reading for Detail:	"Look at what the author says here."
Rereading:	"But if you look back at this part…"
Evaluating:	"I think the most important part is…"

USING THE STRATEGIES		
Strategy Used:		**Date:**
Student or Group	**Student Comments**	**Skills the Comments Indicate**
_____	_____	_____
_____	_____	_____
_____	_____	_____
_____	_____	_____
_____	_____	_____
_____	_____	_____
_____	_____	_____
_____	_____	_____
_____	_____	_____
_____	_____	_____
_____	_____	_____
_____	_____	_____
_____	_____	_____
_____	_____	_____
_____	_____	_____
_____	_____	_____
_____	_____	_____
_____	_____	_____
_____	_____	_____
_____	_____	_____
_____	_____	_____
_____	_____	_____

Strategy: Anticipation Guide

Reading Skill	When can I use this strategy?		
	Prereading	**During Reading**	**Postreading**
Making Predictions	✓		
Using Prior Knowledge	✓		
Analyzing Cause and Effect Relationships		✓	
Analyzing Persuasive Techniques			✓
Making Generalizations			✓

Strategy at a Glance: Anticipation Guide

- The teacher writes the Anticipation Guide, a set of generalizations based on issues in the text and designed to promote discussion and predictions about the selection.
- Students mark whether they agree or disagree with each statement, then discuss their responses.
- While students read, they take notes on the issues in the guide as those issues are revealed in the text.
- After reading, students look at their responses again to see whether they still agree or disagree with the statements.

Both younger and older children do it. They constantly ask what's going on and where they are being taken. They ask what the doctor is going to do before the doctor does it, and they plan what they'll say when they are approaching parents with special requests. Adults do it. We pick up travel brochures before we travel, study maps before we make a car trip, and check out the checkbook before we make a purchase. We all do it—we try to anticipate what's going to happen before it actually happens.

Good readers consciously try to anticipate what a text is about before they begin reading. They look at the cover, art, title, genre, author, headings, graphs, charts, length, print size, inside flaps, and back cover. Some students read the bibliographic information on the copyright page. They ask friends, "Is this any good?" They do anything to find out something about a text before they begin reading.

Struggling readers, on the other hand, often don't do that; they are told to read something, and once the text is in hand, they just begin. They often skip titles and background information, hardly ever read book jackets, and rarely look through the text

Anticipation Guide

for clues. The assignment is to read, so they'll read—maybe. We know they would read better, however, if they brought to reading what they bring to the rest of life: anticipation.

To help students learn to anticipate, use the **Anticipation Guide** strategy. This is a set of generalizations related to the theme of a selection. Students decide whether they agree or disagree with each statement in the guide. These guides activate students' prior knowledge, encourage them to make personal connections to what they will be reading, and give them clues to what the text is about.

Best Uses for Anticipation Guide

An Anticipation Guide (Tierney, Redance, and Dishner 1995) is best used for a topic or issue that students do not know anything about. A major reason for using the guide is to activate students' prior knowledge. If students are about to read something that is outside their experience, then we must build some bridges between their existing experience and the text. That is why the Anticipation Guide is not based on facts but on generalizations students can draw from the text.

Getting the Strategy to Work

1. **First, write the Anticipation Guide.** If you read the text and look for the main ideas or themes that are presented, you will have a start on what will make good items to include in the guide. If one of the issues in the text is survival, jot down generalizations about survival, keeping the most debatable, thought-provoking ones. You do not need a lot of items; two that encourage discussion are better than ten that inspire little debate. Students should mark each statement as one with which they agree or disagree rather than as true or false. You want them to explore what they believe about the statement. The statement might, for example, be one that will open their eyes to aspects of a different culture and at the same time inspire debate ("American schools should follow the European model and not have elective classes students can choose."), or it might be a statement that stimulates discussion because it makes the students think about their own preconceived notions ("Teenagers around the world have the same interests.") Make sure your students understand that you are not looking for a right or wrong answer. For the Anticipation Guide to be effective, students should agree or disagree with the statements.

2. **Introduce the strategy to students.** The best way to teach students how to use an Anticipation Guide is to do one with them. Before reading, students should complete an Anticipation Guide that addresses the issues in the selection. After they have completed the guide and you have talked about their responses, tell students to keep the guide handy as they read, so they can make notes about issues as they are revealed in the text. After students have finished reading, have them look at their original responses to see if their opinions have changed. The reading may have changed their responses by strengthening their original position or by making them doubt that position.

How will students benefit from using this strategy?

- The **Anticipation Guide** strategy encourages students to think about issues and to make predictions.

- It encourages students to make personal connections to what they will read.

- It gives them clues to what the text is about.

- It allows students to look for cause-and-effect relationships.

- It allows students to generalize and to discuss those generalizations.

- It allows students to explore their own responses to a text.

Some Tips for the Most Effective Use of Anticipation Guide

1. Use this strategy as a before-, during-, or after-reading strategy, or as a brainstorming activity for writing, rather than as a pretest or post-test.

2. Use this strategy to activate students' prior knowledge: to build a bridge between their own experiences and the text. The generalizations used in the Anticipation Guide can be drawn from the text.

3. This strategy can be used to promote discussion among the students, or each student can work independently with the generalizations used in the Anticipation Guide. Both methods can be effective, depending on the text selection or the class.

References:

Tierney, Robert J., John E. Readance, and Ernest K. Dishner. 1995. *Reading Strategies and Practices: A Compendium.* 4th ed. Needham Heights, Mass.: Allyn and Bacon.

Strategy: Anticipation Guide

READING: _____

SKILL: _____

I. Before reading the text, read the statements below and decide whether you agree or disagree with each statement. Mark an X in the appropriate space in the *Before Reading* column, and be ready to explain your decision. Then, on the lines below, predict what you think the text will be about.

Before Reading	Statement	After Reading
Agree/Disagree		Agree/Disagree
_____ / _____	1. _____ _____	_____ / _____
_____ / _____	2. _____ _____	_____ / _____
_____ / _____	3. _____ _____	_____ / _____
_____ / _____	4. _____ _____	_____ / _____

My Prediction(s): _____

_____

_____

II. After reading the text, decide if you still agree or disagree with the statements, and mark an X in the appropriate space in the *After Reading* column.

III. Choose three of the Anticipation Guide statements above. On the back of this sheet, describe how each statement relates to the text.

_____

_____

_____

Strategy: It Says ... I Say

Reading Skill	When can I use this strategy?		
	Prereading	During Reading	Postreading
Making Inferences		✓	
Making Generalizations and Drawing Conclusions			✓

Strategy at a Glance: It Says ... I Say

- The teacher creates a model **It Says ... I Say** chart for the classroom. The chart consists of four columns: a question that requires an inference **(Question)**, what the text says about the question **(It Says)**, what students already know about that information **(I Say)**, and their inference **(And So)**.

- The teacher models the strategy using an inferential question based on a familiar story.

- Students practice making inferences by using the chart regularly to explain their answers to inferential questions.

Please read the following: The bridnic scroffelled the ibnic. The ibnic scroffelled the flibberrond. The flibberrond scroffelled the webernet. Now answer the following questions:

1. What did the bridnic scroffell?
2. Did the ibnic scroffell the flibberrond or the bridnic?
3. What scroffelled the webernet?

Here are the answers:

a. The bridnic scroffelled the ibnic.
b. The ibnic scroffelled the flibberrond.
c. The flibberrond scroffelled the webernet.

You were probably able to answer all those questions correctly, because to do so, you didn't have to understand what a *bridnic* or an *ibnic,* or even a *flibberrond,* is. You just needed to match words in the questions to words in the text. But look at the next question:

4. Would you rather be a bridnic, an ibnic, or a flibberrond?

Figuring this one out is more of a problem. You can't answer it until you know what *bridnic, ibnic,* and *flibberrond* mean. And it would probably help a lot to know what *scroffelled* means. Then you could combine what you know about each of those words with what happens to each of those words in the text and draw your own conclusions about which you'd prefer to be. That type of thinking—combining something from the text with something you already know—is called inferential thinking. Skilled readers make inferences as they read; struggling readers often don't. The inability to make inferences creates problems for readers that often result in statements like "I don't get it" and "How'd you know that?" To help students understand how inferences are formed, use a strategy called **It Says ... I Say.** Completing an **It Says ... I Say** chart helps students visualize and internalize the steps of making an inference—combining the information in the text with the information they already know.

Best Uses for It Says ... I Say

Struggling readers spend so much effort just getting the literal details that making an inference as they read is the last thing that happens, if it happens at all. They need a strategy that helps them internalize the process of how to infer. The **It Says ... I Say** chart helps students to see a structure for making an inference.

Getting the Strategy to Work

1. **Introduce the strategy using a short, familiar story.** Ask a few literal questions, and then ask a question that requires students to make an inference. If a student answers it correctly, ask that student to explain how the inference was created using the **It Says ... I Say** chart (see the chart provided on page 9). If no one can answer the question, answer it yourself, writing your responses on the chart.

2. **Model the strategy regularly.** Struggling readers often need multiple models over an extended period of time. But you do not always have to provide the model; have students share their answers to inference questions as another form of modeling.

3. **Quote or paraphrase from the text.** Have students either quote from the text or closely paraphrase it in the **It Says** column. You may also want to look ahead at the questions, think about the answers, and tell students that for a certain question they should find one, two, or three items for their **It Says** column. Eventually, you want students to decide this for themselves, but in the beginning, you might need to provide the support.

4. **Work in groups or pairs.** If you want students to answer a number of questions, you might consider having them work in pairs or small groups. Also, remember that as soon as students can make inferences and tell you how they reached those inferences, they do not need to complete the chart repeatedly. The chart is a scaffold to be used as needed.

How will students benefit from using this strategy?

- Struggling readers are better able to visualize what is happening in the text.
- Readers are better able to visualize the connections between what the text says and what is already in their minds.
- The **It Says … I Say** chart will enable you to "see" students' thinking.
- Students will be able to see the connections they are making.
- Students learn to break down the steps of making an inference.
- Students see what kinds of thinking they need to do.
- Students will internalize the inferencing process and will be able to make inferences without the help of the chart.

Some Tips for the Most Effective Use of It Says … I Say

1. Though students can paraphrase the text in the *It Says* column of their chart, the more directly their comments relate to the text, the better.

2. Look ahead at the questions you want the students to answer, so that the chart does not become too long.

3. Careful selection of questions that require students to make inferences can give them opportunities to develop that critical thinking skill.

4. Some students might need extra guidance in figuring out how many items to list in the *It Says* column. You might need to look ahead at the questions, think about the answers, and tell students that for a certain question, they should find one, two, or three items from the text for their *It Says* column.

5. Use this strategy for students who can't make inferences, in order to teach them how to do it, as well as for students who know how to make inferences but have simply made the wrong inference from the text.

References:

Raphael, Taffy. 1982. Question-Answering Strategies for Children. *The Reading Teacher* 36:186-190.

Name _____ Class _____ Date _____

Strategy: It Says ... I Say

READING: _____

SKILL: _____

Question	It Says (What the text says)	I Say (My thoughts)	And So (My inference)
1.			
2.			
3.			

Strategy: Logographic Cues

Reading Skill	When can I use this strategy?		
	Prereading	During Reading	Postreading
Understanding Text Structure	✓		
Analyzing Chronological Order			✓
Making Generalizations and Understanding Text Structure			✓

Strategy at a Glance: Logographic Cues

- Logographs are graphic representations of ideas. The **Logographic Cues** strategy uses simple pictures that represent or symbolize key ideas in a text.

- Students can use logographs to identify textual elements or organize and remember information.

Dr. Kylene Beers explains the **Logographic Cues** strategy with the following story:

> I sat in the train station in Chaumont, France, wondering why I had taken Latin instead of French in high school and college. At that moment, I wanted to know if my train to Dijon was leaving when I thought it was. Blank stares and pitying shakes of the head were all I received when people realized that I was limited to English. Finally, I took out my map of the region, drew a train, circled my destination, and wrote the date and time of my departure. Underneath it all I put a big question mark. The clerk behind the window finally understood my question: Is the train from Chaumont to Dijon still departing today from this station at 3:48? "Oui," she said, nodding her head.

> Hours later, as I sat on the train, I realized that although I couldn't read French words, I *could* read musical notation, numbers, and international signs. I could read information that was presented logographically, but not information presented alphabetically. A Logographic Cue was worth a million French words.

> "And why not?" I thought. Our first understanding of written language is a logographic understanding. Three- and four-year-olds who recognize their names in print rarely do so because they attach sounds to letters; instead, they simply recognize the shape of their printed names. Logographs, or picture cues, remain helpful when students are confronted with an alphabetic principle or text that they don't understand.

Logographic Cues

The **Logographic Cues** strategy uses simple pictures that represent or symbolize key ideas in a text. Whenever you provide Logographic Cues or let students invent their own cues, their ability to comprehend and remember what they read improves. This simple strategy consistently helps struggling readers connect with text.

Best Use of the Strategy

Students can use logographs as they read to mark important passages and also to provide a visual cue to the meaning of the passage. Some students have a difficult time "seeing" and remembering the events of a text. For these students, picture cues often provide the visual stimulus they need to increase comprehension. Not all students will need to use Logographic Cues as they read a text. Students who don't have difficulty organizing, remembering, or visualizing probably don't need the picture prompt.

Getting the Strategy to Work

Logographic Cues can be used at any time with any text or in any class. Here are some ways students can use logographs with texts, assignment sheets, class notes, and vocabulary. They are a starting point; you'll want to develop your own ways to use Logographic Cues.

1. **Use logographs with novels, short stories, or expository texts.** Logographs can be used as students read a text. Unlike the illustrations in a picture book that illustrate the entire story, Logographic Cues simply provide a broad clue. For many struggling readers, they provide a scaffold to meaning. When using logographs with literature, have students identify basic literary elements, such as setting, characters, conflict, climax, and resolution. Add other literary techniques and stylistic elements to the list as the year progresses. You and your students can decide together which categories to use with a text and which pictures to use to represent those terms you chose. Students may want to draw logographs for literary elements they expect to encounter in the text, while others prefer to wait until they come across a passage that needs to be marked. With students who are really struggling, you might need to point out where to place logographs prior to the reading. Students can also use logographs to illustrate the events in a story and to place those events in the correct chronological sequence.

2. **Use logographs with assignment sheets.** Using Logographic Cues with assignment sheets helps some students understand the assignment sheet so that they can organize and complete them more easily. Students can develop their own system of representing visually different types of assignments. Some examples might be: an open book for a reading assignment, a calendar for long-term assignments, or an open book and pencil for a reading and writing assignment.

3. **Use logographs with classroom notes.** Logographic Cues help students to stay focused while taking notes and to retain more information.

4. **Use logographs with vocabulary study.** Creating logograph cards can help students learn vocabulary words. On one side of the card, students write the vocabulary word; on the other side, they write the definition and draw a logograph that suggests the meaning of the word. A vocabulary logograph can be anything that helps a student remember the meaning of a word, and since this will vary from student to student, it's important that students always create their own logographs for vocabulary.

How can students benefit from this strategy?

- Logographs can increase comprehension for some students.

- As students decide what symbol would best represent an idea in the text, they are encouraged to think critically about what they are reading.

- Logographs are an effective organizational tool.

Some Tips for the Most Effective Use of Logographic Cues

1. Do not think that logographs replace text with pictures and therefore encourage students not to read. A logograph is a step into the text, not a replacement for the text.

2. When students first use this strategy, they may need to use logographs that you or other students have prepared earlier. But they should be encouraged to create their own as soon as possible.

3. If students don't want to use the logographs but are having trouble visualizing the ideas in the text, they might be afraid that they don't draw well enough. Remind them that logographs are not pieces of art. They are graphics intended to help as text organizers or as an aid to comprehension.

4. Logographs should not be graded. Use them to assess what students have learned from the text, or, if using them with vocabulary words, to assess students' understanding of the new words.

5. Logographs can be especially helpful when students are dealing with complicated content. The symbols they create can help them sort out the content and more quickly understand it.

Strategy: Logographic Cues

READING: _____

SKILL: _____

Logographic Cues

Strategy: Most Important Word

Reading Skill	When can I use this strategy?		
	Prereading	During Reading	Postreading
Identifying the Main Idea			✓
Making Generalizations			✓
Summarizing			✓

Strategy at a Glance: Most Important Word

- After reading a text, students discuss their responses to the theme of the work.
- Students decide either independently or in small groups what they think the Most Important Word in the text is, basing their answers on evidence from the reading.
- Students share and explain their choices.

Many times when you ask students to find the main idea of a story, or to make a generalization, or simply, "What message are you carrying away from this story?", they can't do it, because they find the question too broad, too open. One strategy that students can use to help them answer the question is **Most Important Word. Most Important Word** is a postreading strategy in which students decide which word in a text they think is the most important based on specific evidence in the text. As students decide which word is the most important, they begin to formulate their responses to the question, " What did the story mean to you?" **Most Important Word** leads to revealing discussions that cause students to use those skills as they read and reflect on what they have read.

Best Use of the Strategy

Most Important Word (Bleich 1975) is a good strategy to help students identify the theme of a reading and to make generalizations about it by breaking down the selection and deciding which word in the text carries the message that speaks to them.

Getting the Strategy to Work

1. **Introduce the strategy.** Model this strategy by reading a short text, such as a picture book or a poem, and then by talking through how you decided which word was the most important. Refer to specific evidence in the text to support your opinions.

2. **Discuss the selection.** Give students time to discuss the story before you ask them what the Most Important Word is. Let them respond to parts of the text that they liked or didn't like, that they didn't understand, or that remind them of something else.

3. **Allow adequate time for students to make their choices.** If you really want students to find what they consider to be the Most Important Word, you must give them time to find that word.

Provide opportunities for students to share and explain their choices. Students can explain their choice of the Most Important Word in an essay or in several other ways. They might work in small groups to share their choices of Most Important Word, explain their reasoning, listen to responses, and then make comments in return. It is a good exercise to have a small group come to a consensus on which word they, as a group, consider the Most Important Word. You can also ask students to think about the text outside of class and come up with the Most Important Word. Tell students that they may not choose a character's name as the Most Important Word. Some students are inclined to select a name as they read a book through the main character's eyes and live out all the action from that character's point of view.

For students who are overwhelmed by this assignment and choose an article, conjunction, or similar word as the Most Important Word, you may want to modify the assignment. Have them find the most important chapter, passage, or scene, and then narrow their focus to the most important sentence, and finally, to the Most Important Word.

How will students benefit from this strategy?

- The **Most Important Word** strategy helps students decide which word in a text they think is the most important based on specific evidence in the text.

- As students decide which word in the text is the most important, they begin to formulate their responses to the question, "What did this story mean to you?"

- Looking for the Most Important Word leads to meaningful discussions about the message of the text.

- This strategy improves the students' abilities to summarize, recognize cause-and-effect relationships, identify main ideas, and make inferences and generalizations.

Some Tips for the Most Effective Use of Most Important Word

1. It is sometimes helpful to have students think first on their own about what they consider the Most Important Word, before they discuss it in a group. You can group students in two different ways: put students who picked the same word in respective groups, or have groups in which each student has chosen a different Most Important Word. In the first grouping, students can discuss the different reasons for having selected that word as the Most Important Word.

2. Students should select a word that comes from the text, rather than a word that is not mentioned in the text but that comes to mind when thinking about the text.

3. Tell students not to use a character's name as the Most Important Word. They may see the text through that character's eyes, but that will not necessarily lead them to understanding the most important idea in the text.

4. Remember that some students will find this activity overwhelming and will do better if they first find the most important chapter, passage, or scene, and then narrow it down to the most important word.

References:

Bleich, David. 1975. *Readings and Feelings: An Introduction to Subjective Criticism.* Urbana, Illinois: National Council of Teachers of English.

Strategy: Most Important Word

READING: _____

SKILL: _____

I. After reading the text, review it and choose three words that you think are important. In the chart below, write each word in the left-hand column. In the right-hand column, explain why you think each word may be the most important. Use examples from the text to support each word choice.

Important Words	Why This Word Is Important in the Text
1.	
2.	
3.	

II. Look at the chart above and the reasons for each word choice. Then, complete the following items on the lines provided.

4. After thinking about your word choices in Part 1, what do you think the Most Important Word in this text is?

_____

5. How does this word relate to the text?

_____

_____

III. In a small group, share and discuss the Most Important Words chosen by members of the group. What do you think about the words chosen by other group members? Do you agree or disagree with their reasons for choosing their words? After you have finished your discussion, complete the following items on the lines provided.

6. After my group's discussion, I think _____ is the Most Important Word.

7. I changed / didn't change my mind because _____

_____

Strategy: Probable Passage

Reading Skill	When can I use this strategy?		
	Prereading	**During Reading**	**Postreading**
Identifying Purpose	✓		✓
Making Predictions	✓		
Comparing and Contrasting			✓

Strategy at a Glance: Probable Passage

- The teacher chooses key words or phrases from the text students will read, then develops categories for the words and writes the Probable Passage (a cloze passage with key words omitted).

- Before students read the text, they arrange the key words and phrases in the categories. Then they fill in the blanks in the cloze passage with the key words.

- After students read the text, they discuss how their passages were similar to or different from the actual text.

Many readers struggle because they don't predict what a selection might be about and don't think about what they already know about a topic. These students simply open a book, look at words, and begin turning pages. **Probable Passage** is a strategy that helps stop those poor reading habits by encouraging students to make predictions and to activate their prior knowledge about a topic.

Best Use of the Strategy

Probable Passage (Wood 1984) is a brief preview of a text from which key words and phrases have been omitted. The teacher chooses these key words from the text and presents them to the students. In some cases, it might be necessary to discuss the meaning of the words; many times, students can figure this out for themselves. Students arrange the words in categories according to their probable functions in the story (such as Setting, Characters, or Conflicts), then use the words to fill in the blanks of the Probable Passage. After reading the story, students compare it to their passages and discuss differences. As students work through this process, they use what they know about story structure, think about vocabulary, practice making predictions, and compare their predictions to the story line.

Probable Passage

Getting the Strategy to Work

1. **First, choose key words and write the Probable Passage.** After reading a story, choose the key words, think about what categories are needed, and design a Probable Passage (a cloze passage). To choose key words, it is easiest to work backward: write the Probable Passage, then choose the key words and develop the categories. Some possible categories: Setting, Characters, Problem, Resolution; or Conflict, Solution, Resolution, Climax; or Causes and Effects, Problems and Solutions. Be careful not to select too many key words. More than fifteen is usually too many, and fewer than eight is usually not enough.

2. **Then, model the strategy a few times.** This means that students need to see you thinking about words, placing them in the correct category, and using them in the Probable Passage. After reading the story, they need to see you discuss how the passage affected your reading of the story.

3. **Use Probable Passage before and after reading a selection.** Students begin by arranging the key words into the categories you have provided. After categorizing the key words, students place them within the cloze passage. At that point, they might change the way they have categorized the words. Students then read the text. Some may want to keep their passages with them as they read. After reading, students compare their paragraph with the text and either revise their passages or just discuss the differences.

Probable Passage is a powerful prereading strategy that encourages students to make predictions and to activate their prior knowledge, and it also serves as a postreading discussion tool.

How will students benefit from using this strategy?

- This strategy helps less proficient readers learn how to use their prior experiences to help them predict what might happen.

- Students learn to look closely at new vocabulary, think about the words in relationship to the story, and fit them into a Probable Passage before seeing them in the text.

- Comparison of students' predictions with what happened in the story leads to some interesting discussions.

- Talking about the skills targeted with this strategy helps struggling readers to see the "invisible" things that good readers do, such as making predictions, modifying their predictions as they read, and making connections between the text and what they already know.

Some Tips for the Most Effective Use of Probable Passage

1. When selecting the words to be used in the Probable Passage, keep in mind that fifteen is probably too many, and fewer than eight is probably not enough. Read the text first, select important vocabulary words, think about the Probable Passage frame, and decide on the categories. This process will lead you to the words that students should know.

2. This strategy is most effective with students who need more structure when they attempt to read a new text. It will help them examine the vocabulary more closely and think about the words in relation to the story.

3. Don't skip the step of having students compare their choices for the Probable Passage with the actual text. Comparing the two will lead to some interesting discussions about their predictions.

4. This strategy very effectively helps struggling readers see the things that readers do in order to understand a text, such as making predictions, modifying their predictions as they read, and making connections between the text and what they already know.

5. When preparing a Probable Passage, keep the categories broad, use phrases as needed, and make sure the passage uses words that fit in the categories.

References:

Wood, Karen D. 1984. Probable Passages: A Writing Strategy. *The Reading Teacher* 37: 496-499.

Strategy: Probable Passage

READING: _____

SKILL: _____

Study the following words and phrases and arrange them into the categories below. Then, referring to your categorized list when necessary, complete the Probable Passage provided to you by your teacher.

Key Words

_____

_____

_____

Categories for Sorting Words and Phrases			

_____

_____

_____

_____

_____

_____

_____

_____

My Probable Passage is different from the text.

My Probable Passage _____

_____

but the text _____

_____

Strategy: Read, Rate, Reread

Reading Skill	When can I use this strategy?		
	Prereading	During Reading	Postreading
Making Inferences		✓	
Identifying the Main Idea		✓	
Determining the Writer's Purpose			✓

Strategy at a Glance: Read, Rate, Reread

- Students read a short text three times, rating their understanding of the text and writing down any questions they have after each reading.

- After the third reading, students discuss with a partner or in a small group any unanswered questions. Then students rate their understanding a fourth and final time.

- As a class, students discuss how their ratings changed between readings, as well as asking any questions they still have.

Many struggling readers don't think reading the same passage or text again does them any good. That is partly because they operate under the misconception that other readers read something once, read it somewhat effortlessly, and "get it" every time, the first time. Rereading doesn't look any different from reading, so struggling readers don't see how many times proficient readers pause, loop back a few sentences, reread up to a point, reflect, start over completely, and then perhaps proceed slowly. Moreover, as we discuss texts with students, we rarely bring up the issue of *how* to understand; we are too busy focusing on *what* students understand. Therefore, struggling readers don't hear teachers or other students talk about the words—or even chapters—that they sometimes reread several times before formulating a meaning. We need to help these students understand that rereading is something good readers do and that it is an important strategy to use when trying to understand a text.

Best Use of the Strategy

Use this strategy to offer students concrete evidence that comprehension does improve with repeated reading. We often tell students that rereading will increase their understanding of a text, but struggling readers need proof. They have years of evidence that reading does not work; therefore, they reason, why would rereading work any better? The structure provided by the **Read, Rate, Reread** strategy (Blau 1992)— the rating and questioning —provides the proof.

Getting the Strategy to Work

1. **First, model the strategy.** A good way to model the strategy is by actually bringing in a short text, such as a poem with which you are unfamiliar. Read it aloud to the class, rate your understanding, think through your questions, and then repeat the process. Students see you rereading and hear you making sense of the text.

2. **Then, choose a text for students to read and reread.** The text should be short enough for students to complete this process in one class period. Make sure that the text is accessible enough for understanding to increase with repeated readings, as it is important that students see their ratings ultimately go up as they reread.

3. **Have students read the text three times, rating their understanding and writing down questions they have about the text after each reading.** Tell students to read the text for the first time and rate their understanding on a scale of one to ten, and write any questions they have after the first reading. Suggest that students slow down during the second reading, especially on the parts they did not understand. As they record their second rating, they can eliminate any questions they can now answer and write down any new ones they may have. They should read the selection for a third time, record their rating, and again eliminate questions or jot down new ones.

4. **After the third reading, have students discuss any unanswered questions.** Have them work with a partner or a small group to see if they can answer any of the questions they still have and then rate their understanding after their discussion. Later, students can move from writing questions to making connections and predictions. Eventually they can move to writing responses.

5. **Discuss how students' scores changed.** Generally, students will see an upward trend, though some students will see that the second or third reading actually leaves them more confused than the first reading. These students are often the ones who are really thinking while reading. Because the text is more familiar the second or third time, they discover things they overlooked or misunderstood the first time. The rating of their understanding is lower because they are now aware of what they do not understand. What you want students to remember is that asking questions about what they are reading, and then rereading to answer those questions, will increase their understanding of a text.

6. **Finally, leave time for students to discuss as a class any questions they still cannot answer.** These questions are usually very interesting and open-ended, and the discussions that emerge are often lively and take the class back into the text. The questions generally require inferential thinking, and as students discuss possible answers, they see how inferences are formed.

Read, Rate, Reread

How will students benefit by using this strategy?

- This strategy demonstrates to students that they can understand more about a text by rereading.

- Students feel empowered and they are more aware readers because they see that they can improve their understanding of a text.

- By providing students a tool that enables them to assess their understanding of a text, this strategy helps students to become proficient readers.

Some Tips for the Most Effective Use of Read, Rate, Reread

1. It is important that students do all of the steps in this strategy in order to use it effectively. Students should: 1) rate their level of understanding with each reading; 2) write down questions that they first try to answer and then discuss with a partner; and 3) rate themselves one final time in order to see that their understanding has improved.

2. Text selection for this strategy is crucial: students must care about being successful in understanding it, and it should not be too difficult. It should be a text that students will understand better with repeated readings.

3. Once students learn how to use this strategy, they can use it effectively both at home, as homework, and in other classes, such a social studies and science.

4. It is better not to grade students' ratings and the questions they generate, on the assumption that every question that comes out of their reading is a valuable question.

5. When first learning to use this strategy, students may need to be told which portions of a text to reread, and how often to use this strategy. But gradually they will learn this for themselves. Since students will eventually be rereading different texts or portions of texts, the discussion of their ratings and any unanswered questions can take place through journal writing, where you can also respond to any questions they still have.

6. Make sure students understand that the process is the important thing in this strategy. A 10 rating is not as important as growth, which should demonstrate to students that they can understand more about a text by rereading it.

References:

Blau, Sheridan. 1992. The Writing Process and the Teacher of Literature. Keynote address given at the annual meeting of the Greater Dallas Council of Teachers of English, 15 February, 1992, Fort Worth, Texas.

Name _____ Class _____ Date _____

Strategy: Read, Rate, Reread

READING: _____

SKILL: _____

Read the text and rate your understanding of it on a scale of 1 to 10. (A score of 1 means you didn't understand it at all; a score of 10 means you understood it completely.) Record your rating in the *First Rating* box. Then, on the lines provided for item 1 below, write any questions you have after your first reading. Repeat this process two more times (items 2 and 3). Then, discuss any unanswered questions with a partner and rate your understanding a fourth time.

First Rating	Second Rating	Third Rating	Fourth Rating

1. Write down any questions you have after the **first** reading. Use the back of this paper to continue writing if necessary.

   _____

   _____

   _____

2. Read the text a **second** time and record your rating in the *Second Rating* box. Slow down at the parts you didn't understand the first time you read. Then cross out any questions you can now answer. Write down any new questions you have after the second reading.

   _____

   _____

   _____

3. Read the text a **third** time and record your rating in the *Third Rating* box. Cross out any questions you can now answer. Write down any new questions you have after the third reading.

   _____

   _____

   _____

4. After the third reading, get with a partner and see if the two of you can answer any of the questions you both still have. Cross out any questions you answer. Then rate your understanding a fourth time and record your rating in the *Fourth Rating* box.

Strategy: Retellings

Reading Skill	When can I use this strategy?		
	Prereading	**During Reading**	**Postreading**
Analyzing Chronological Order			✓
Identifying the Main Idea			✓
Summarizing			✓

Strategy at a Glance: Retellings

- The teacher models the strategy by reading a brief story and retelling it to students. Then the class evaluates and discusses the teacher's Retelling using a rubric.

- Using a rubric, students plan and evaluate their Retellings.

- The teacher assesses students' progress over time by plotting their scores on a chart.

A student is asked to tell what happened in a story, and the answer might sound something like this: "Well, there was this guy ... and he, well he and his brother, they ... well, then they leave ... and then some stuff happens." While the general notion of "stuff happens" in a story is accurate, the phrase seems to lack the specificity most of us want in a discussion of a reading text—or a piece of literature. But this level of summary is what many students offer us on a regular basis. The **Retellings** strategy is a good way to move students past the "stuff happens" response. A Retelling is an oral summary of a text based on a set of story elements, such as setting, main characters, and conflicts. Students use Retellings to help them become more specific in their summarizing.

Best Use of the Strategy

The **Retellings** strategy (Tierney, Readence, and Dishner 1995) provides a structure for students who have difficulty recalling what they have read and retelling the information in a logical and coherent manner. Using Retellings effectively means modeling them often, giving students a rubric they can use to plan and evaluate Retellings, evaluating students' Retellings over time so students can see growth and areas that need work, and finally, using students' Retellings as a way to plan your instruction.

Getting the Strategy to Work

1. **Model several Retellings.** Begin by reading a short story or a picture book to students; then, retell it. You'll need to have looked over the rubric you want to use and to have practiced this Retelling. Next, put a copy of the rubric you want students to

use on the overhead projector and discuss your Retelling with students. Model a Retelling every day for several days, letting students score them. Even after students begin giving their own Retellings, continue modeling Retellings from time to time.

2. **Use a rubric to plan and evaluate Retellings.** An example of a **Retellings** rubric appears on page 28. You can adopt this rubric for your students or write your own. What is important is that students see the rubric before they give their Retellings. You might let students use the rubric as they give their Retellings.

You may have students work in pairs and rate each other's Retellings. Have students read the first section of the text. One partner should retell this part of the selection while the other (the listener) scores the Retelling using the rubric. Then students read the last section of the text and switch roles for the retelling and scoring of the conclusion of the selection.

3. **Evaluate students' progress over time.** To chart progress in a meaningful way, assess the Retellings and plot them on a chart, using the same rubric each time. To reduce the number of Retellings you listen to, think about who needs to do Retellings. Students who can find the main idea and supporting details, organize thoughts about a text, and relate events in the correct sequence do not need this strategy. You do not have to listen to all your students' Retellings; one or two a month should be enough. But students should practice Retellings often. The more often they have a chance to practice the strategy, the better the results. At other times, let students score each other's Retellings or score their own from recordings they make.

How will students benefit from using this strategy?

Students use Retellings

- to help them become more specific in their summarizing

- to become more organized

- to discover main ideas and supporting details

- to become aware of their audience, use of language, and personal responses to texts.

Some Tips for the Most Effective Use of Retellings

1. Once students understand how to use Retellings, you can have them write them in order to practice their writing skills.

2. Limit the number of students who use this strategy at one time. Focus on those who need to learn to find the main idea and organize their thoughts about a text.

3. When students are learning to use this strategy, the more often they have a chance to do Retellings, the better the results. Although you will need to model for the students less and less often, it is important to model the Retelling of new text types that they encounter.

References:

Tierney, Robert J., John E. Readence, and Ernest K. Dishner. 1995. *Reading Strategies and Practices: A Compendium.* 4th ed. Needham Heights, Mass.: Allyn and Bacon.

Strategy: Retellings

READING: _____

SKILL: _____

Retellings Rubric

Name _____ Date _____

Text _____ Selected by _____

Directions: Use the following checklist to rate the Retelling. For each item below, circle a number from 0-3 in the appropriate column. On this scale, 0 means the Retelling doesn't include the item at all, and 3 means the Retelling completely and successfully includes the item.

Does this Retelling

1. have an introduction that includes the story's title and setting?   0   1   2   3

2. give the characters' names and explain how the characters are related to one another?   0   1   2   3

3. identify the antagonists and protagonists?   0   1   2   3

4. include the main events?   0   1   2   3

5. keep the main events in the correct sequence?   0   1   2   3

6. provide supporting details?   0   1   2   3

7. make sense?   0   1   2   3

8. sound organized?   0   1   2   3

9. discuss the main conflict / problem in the story?   0   1   2   3

10. explain how the main conflict / problem was resolved?   0   1   2   3

11. connect the story to another story or to the reader's life?   0   1   2   3

12. include the reader's personal response to the story?   0   1   2   3

Total Score _____

Comments from listener about the Retelling:

Suggestions for the next Retelling:

Strategy: Retellings

READING: _____

SKILL: _____

Name _____ Class _____

Retellings Progress Chart

R13									
R12									
R11									
R10									
R9									
R8									
R7									
R6									
R5									
R4									
R3									
R2									
R1									
	Sept	Oct	Nov	Dec	Jan	Feb	Mar	Apr	May

Strategy: Save the Last Word for Me

Reading Skill	When can I use this strategy?		
	Prereading	During Reading	Postreading
Comparing and Contrasting			✓
Determining the Main Idea			✓

Strategy at a Glance: Save the Last Word for Me

- After reading a text, students prepare a **Last Word** card: they write their favorite passage from the text on the front of the card; on the back of the card, they write why they like that passage.

- In small groups, students take turns reading their selected passages. The others in the group give their response to the passage.

- After everyone has finished making comments, each student reads his or her comments about the passage, thus having the "last word" about the passage.

Some readers struggle through texts, and when they have finished, they have nothing to say about what they have read. Maybe it's because they never seem to get it right. No one wants to be told continually that their answers are wrong, so rather than speak up in class about what they have read, they just proclaim that they have nothing to say. They either can't answer the question ("What do you want to say about the story?") or they risk an answer, only to discover that their answer is wrong. Eventually, they learn to distrust their own responses, and finally, they don't even bother to form them. When that happens, these readers must be convinced to trust their ability to form responses and to recognize that all readers—including good readers—constantly refine their responses based on what they already know, what they learn from the text, and from others. A strategy that helps readers learn to trust their own responses while learning from others' responses is called **Save the Last Word for Me.** This strategy requires students to choose a portion of a text that they particularly like and to copy that text onto the front of a note card. On the back of the card, they explain what that sentence or passage means to them. Next, students get into small groups and share their passages. The listeners respond to the passage by saying what it means to them. After everyone has finished making comments, the student who wrote the comment turns the card over and shares what he or she has written. At that point, no one can refute, add to, change, or argue with what is said. The last word belongs to that student. Students are willing to participate in **Save the Last Word for Me** because it allows each voice to be heard and, at the same time, gives each participant the opportunity to be the authority.

Best Use of the Strategy

Use the **Save the Last Word For Me** strategy (Short, Harste, and Burke 1996) to encourage struggling readers to do something they rarely do: find a passage in a text that is meaningful to them, listen to what others have to say about the text, and then offer their opinions unchallenged. For students who have rarely given themselves the opportunity to volunteer any response, **Save the Last Word For Me** provides a safety net that encourages risk taking. But the strategy does much more than improve students' confidence. As students look for the passage that is meaningful to them, they are rereading, comparing and contrasting, and learning to articulate why a given passage is meaningful.

Getting the Strategy to Work

1. **First, explain the strategy by actually doing it with students.** Before you begin a discussion of a text with your students, prepare a **Last Word** card. On the front, write your favorite sentence or passage from the text; on the back, explain why you chose that passage and why you think it is significant. Then read the passage to the students and give them a chance to react to it. When they have finished, tell them that you are going to read aloud what you have to say about the passage (your reason for selecting it). Then read the passage on the card and ask students to comment.

2. **Second, have your students prepare their Last Word cards.** They can use either the same story that you used to model the strategy or another story. You might consider having students identify the important passage at home and then discuss it in class.

3. **Third, have students share their passages and comments.** Since the focus of this strategy is to let students have the last word, they will need in-class time for discussions. Reading, choosing passages, and preparing cards can be done outside of class, but the sharing and responding must be done in class. Because this strategy is a good prewriting strategy, you might sometimes have students write their responses, using their own initial comments as well as what other students have said about their passages. These written responses can then be evaluated. You can also evaluate the strategy by giving a participation grade, looking at students' passages and responses on their cards, and comparing their responses over time.

How will students benefit from using this strategy?

- **Save the Last Word for Me** gives struggling readers the chance to form responses without the worry of being told they are wrong.

- It also encourages them to look closely at a text, choose a part that is meaningful to them, listen to what others say about their choice, and articulate first in writing and then orally why that text is important to them.

Some Tips for the Most Effective Use of Save the Last Word for Me

1. Have students write down their responses. Students should commit their thoughts to paper. Without that commitment, they often write down a passage without figuring out why they like it.

2. It is all right if students change their mind about their selection after they hear the opinions of other students. It means that they are listening to and learning from others, and it has the added bonus of getting them to explain how listening to another student affected their thinking.

3. To avoid having students simply pick any passage and say they "just liked it," require them to state at least two reasons why they selected that passage.

4. If a student still wants to say something after someone has had the last word, you should hold firm in not allowing them to do that. To do otherwise takes away some of the benefit of the strategy. If you decide to modify that, make sure you and your students are aware that you have modified the strategy.

References:

Short, Kathy Gnagey, Jerome C. Harste, and Carolyn L. Burke. 1996. *Creating Classrooms for Authors and Inquirers.* 2nd ed. Portsmouth, N. H.: Heinemann Publishers.

Strategy: Save the Last Word for Me

READING: _____

SKILL: _____

I. After reading the text, look back through it and choose what you consider the most important word in the text. Then, complete the following statements on the lines provided.

   1. The most important word in the text is _____.

   2. List several reasons for choosing this word. Be sure that your reasons are supported with

      examples directly from the text. _____

      _____

      _____

      _____

      _____

      _____

      _____

II. Discuss the most important word with a partner. Write down your partner's choice and his or her reason for choosing it. Discuss the two choices and try to agree on the most important word in the text.

   1. My partner's choice for most important word: _____

   2. His or her reasons for choosing this word: _____

      _____

      _____

      _____

   3. My partner and I agree that the most important word is _____

      because _____

      _____

      _____

      _____

      _____

Strategy: Say Something

Reading Skill	When can I use this strategy?		
	Prereading	During Reading	Postreading
Using Prior Knowledge (Drawing from Your Own Experience)	✓		
Monitoring Reading		✓	

Strategy at a Glance: Say Something

- The teacher models the strategy by "saying something" about a text with a colleague or by reading and discussing a typed **Say Something** dialogue with students.

- Students read a short text, stopping occasionally to discuss the text with a partner. In their conversations, they must make a prediction, ask a question, make a comment, or make a connection.

- Students practice **Say Something** using very short texts before using the strategy with longer assignments.

Often readers are unable to discuss something they just read because while they read, their eyes move over the words, but their minds move to thoughts of weekend plans, last night's phone conversations, or after-school sports events. They don't focus on what they are reading. To help students break that habit, we need to help them pay attention to what they are reading. **Say Something** is a very simple strategy that keeps readers focused on a text. **Say Something** helps students think about what they are reading by helping them see where they aren't paying attention.

Best Use of the Strategy

Say Something (Horste, Short, and Burke 1988) is a strategy in which students occasionally pause and "say something" to a partner about what they have read. This strategy helps students comprehend what they are reading by helping them to stay focused. Telling students to say something about the text, or giving them specific types of things they can say, keeps them interacting with the text. From that interaction comes meaning.

Getting the Strategy to Work

1. **First, model the strategy.** In order to model the **Say Something** strategy, it is best if you can recruit a colleague to help you demonstrate the strategy. Read aloud each piece of text you will comment on to the students, so they can understand what you say about it. Make sure you say a range of things—from asking very specific

questions, such as how to say a certain word, to making very general comments, such as saying what the passage reminds you of.

2. **Explain the rules to students.** After you model the **Say Something** strategy, go over the rules until students get the idea of how to use the strategy. The rules include the following:

Rules for Say Something
1. With your partner, decide who will say something first.
2. When you say something, you may do one of the following:
   make a prediction
   ask a question
   make a comment
   make a connection
3. If you can't do one of those four things, then you need to reread.

You can explain the response categories by telling them the following:

When you do your **Say Somethings,** there are four things you can say.

1. You can say what you think may happen next. That's called a prediction. You make a prediction by saying, for example, "I think that ... will happen." or "I predict that ..."

2. You can ask a question. If you don't know a word, don't understand a sentence, or feel confused about what is happening, then ask a question. ("What do you think that means?" or "Why does ... say that?")

3. If you don't want to make a prediction or ask a question, then you can make a comment. This can be a comment about what you like or don't like, what you don't understand, what you think is interesting, or what you think about what is happening. ("I like ... because ..." or "I don't know why ... said that.")

4. Finally, you can make a connection. That means you can say, "That reminds me of ..." or "This story is like ..." or "This person makes me think of ...."

You can either choose the points in the text where you want students to stop and say something or have students decide. Tell students that when they stop (after every three or four paragraphs), they must say one of the four things stated in the rules.

2. **Provide opportunities for practice.** Students first need to practice using **Say Something** on very short texts. You may wish to use a chart to help students keep track of how many predictions, comments, questions, or connections they make. Students may also use this strategy without a partner using a variation in which they plan where they will stop and say something to themselves or write something about what they have just read.

How will students benefit from using this strategy?

- The goal of the **Say Something** strategy is to increase students' understanding of the text by helping them pay attention to the text.

- Having students stop to make comments or ask questions about what they are reading engages them in a dialogue with the text.

- As a result of this conversation, students create meaning.

- When students use this strategy, they learn that if they don't have anything to say about a text, they need to go back and reread it because they missed something.

Some Tips for the Most Effective Use of Say Something

1. When setting up pairs for this strategy, it's a good idea to let students choose their own partners. Students at their age are so connected to their friends that putting them together with someone they never spend time with almost assures failure for the strategy.

2. This strategy is most helpful for students who have trouble staying focused.

3. It is difficult to put a letter or number grade on a Say Something, but you can give students points or grades for participation. You might also want to have them evaluate the value of this strategy themselves by occasionally asking them these questions:
   - How has using Say Something changed how you read?
   - What's something you discovered through Say Something about the story you just finished?
   - What types of comments do you make the least often and the most often?
   - What do you want to do to make your Say Somethings more effective?
   - What do you need me to do to help you with your Say Somethings?

4. Say Something can be done alone or with a partner, at school or at home. Silent Say Something provides students with feedback where a partner isn't available and is particularly helpful as an independent reading strategy.

5. Have students stop to make comments or ask questions about what they are reading. This is a means of engaging them in a dialogue with the text and hence, creating meaning.

References:

Harste, Jerome C., Kathy Gnagey Short, and Carolyn L. Burke. 1988. *Creating Classrooms for Authors: The Reading-Writing Connection.* Portsmouth, N.H.: Heinemann Publishers.

Strategy: Say Something

READING: _____

SKILL: _____

SAY SOMETHING CHART			
Prediction	**Comment**	**Question**	**Connection**

Strategy: Sketch to Stretch

Reading Skill	When can I use this strategy?		
	Prereading	During Reading	Postreading
Drawing Conclusions			✓
Making Generalizations			✓
Analyzing Cause and Effect			✓
Summarizing			✓

Strategy at a Glance: Sketch to Stretch

- The teacher introduces **Sketch to Stretch** to students by showing and discussing symbolic pictures based on a text.

- After reading a selection, students work independently or with a partner to create their own symbolic sketches. On the back of the sketches, students write why they drew what they did, using evidence from the text to support their opinions.

- Students share their sketches in small groups, allowing others to comment before revealing their explanations of their work.

Many students find it difficult to go beyond the reading selection to talk about the theme, or the symbolism, or to express a generalization about the story that can be applied to their lives. But some students who have difficulty talking about a text can express their ideas visually, far beyond what even they themselves imagine. This strategy, **Sketch to Stretch**, gives students the opportunity to formulate images that represent the ideas they cannot otherwise express. For some students, putting ideas into pictures, rather than words, is the best way to express their responses to the text.

This is a postreading strategy in which students think about what a passage or entire selection means to them and then draw symbolic representations of their interpretations of the text. As students discuss the text and decide what to draw, they think about the theme, draw conclusions, form generalizations, recognize cause-and-effect relationships, and summarize.

Best Use of the Strategy

Using this strategy to help students use critical thinking skills while they read will encourage them to recognize cause-and-effect relationships, identify the main idea, make inferences, draw conclusions, and form generalizations. The more they use these skills, the more automatic the critical thinking becomes. Eventually, **Sketch to Stretch** (Harste and Burke 1988) is not needed as a way to encourage good reading and can instead be used simply as a springboard to discussion. For either purpose, the strategy encourages closer examination of the text and what it means to the reader.

Getting the Strategy to Work

1. **Introduce the strategy to students.** First, show students some symbolic pictures based on a text. Until you have a group of illustrations former students have made, you will need to create some. As you discuss the pictures, make sure students understand that the drawings are symbolic representations of what the story means to them and not literal illustrations of events from the story.

2. **Then, have students create their sketches and write explanations of their choices.** After students have read the selection, let them work alone or with a partner to create a sketch. If working with a partner, students can either arrive at a consensus about what to draw, or draw individual sketches. When they have finished their sketches, have students write their explanations of why they drew what they did on the back of the drawings. Encourage students to use evidence from the text to support their opinions.

3. **Finally, have students share their sketches.** Divide the class into groups to share their sketches and remind students to let others respond to the sketch before they explain it themselves. Often a response to the sketch triggers a better discussion than the explanation of it. Some students may consistently want to create literal representations of a scene in the text; this may be an indication that they are still thinking at a concrete-operational rather than an abstract-reasoning stage. Continue to model examples of what symbolic pictures look like and also keep those students working with partners so that discussion takes place. Remind students who insist they cannot draw that realistic art is not necessary. Choose sketches that are strong symbolically but simply drawn to reinforce this point.

How will students benefit from using this strategy?

- Because the strategy requires students to draw a symbolic picture, they find themselves rereading the text, thinking about events in the story and what caused them, and drawing conclusions.

- When asked to draw symbolically, students have to think at an abstract level. As a result, they begin to make inferences and generalizations.

Sketch to Stretch

Some Tips for the Most Effective Use of Sketch to Stretch

1. For students who have a hard time thinking in abstract terms as opposed to literal terms, it's best to continue to model examples of what symbolic pictures look like and to keep those students working with a partner, so that a lot of discussion can take place.

2. For some students, the task of drawing a sketch after reading a whole section or novel can be overwhelming. To help them move ahead, suggest points throughout the text where they might want to stop and make a sketch. By breaking the material up into smaller chunks, students have less to think about and as a result find cause-and-effect relationships, determine the main idea, draw conclusions, and make generalizations.

3. To encourage students who lack artistic talent, avoid showing only well-drawn sketches as models. Instead, choose sketches that are strong in symbolic meaning, even though they may be simplistic. Often, a student will say that he or she can't draw. Emphasize that this activity is about *sketching,* not about producing a completed piece of art!

4. Sketch to Stretch may be used with nonfiction, fiction, poems, novels, and expository and narrative writing.

5. This strategy is most effective when used as a postreading strategy. However students can also create sketches as they are reading. Occasionally, a sketch may be shown as a means of introducing the text, and then the sketch can be discussed further in depth after the reading.

6. Students should include a written explanation at the bottom of their sketches or on the back. This helps students express the symbolism of the sketch in writing and enables the rest of the class to better understand what the sketch means to the student who drew it.

References:

Harste, Jerome C. and Carolyn L. Burke, 1988. *Creating Classrooms for Authors.* Portsmouth, N.H. Heinemann Publishers.

Strategy: Sketch to Stretch

READING: _____

SKILL: _____

Directions After reading the text, draw a symbolic sketch in the space below that represents a conclusion you made based on the text.

On the lines below, write an explanation of your sketch. Then, write your conclusions, using specific evidence from the text to support your conclusions.

My Explanation:

_____

_____

_____

_____

_____

My Conclusions:

_____

_____

_____

_____

_____

Strategy: Somebody Wanted But So

Reading Skill	When can I use this strategy?		
	Prereading	During Reading	Postreading
Analyzing Cause and Effect Relationships			✓
Summarizing			✓

Strategy at a Glance: Somebody Wanted But So

- After students read a story, they work alone or in groups to fill in columns on the **Somebody Wanted But So** chart: who the <u>someone</u> in the story is, what he or she <u>wanted</u>, <u>but</u> what happened that created a problem, and <u>so</u> how the problem was resolved.

- Students work together to condense **Somebody Wanted But So** statements into concise summaries or to develop summaries for longer texts.

- To focus on literary elements, students can write **Somebody Wanted But So** statements for different characters in the same story or for different types of conflicts.

Summarizing a short story or a novel appears to be too overwhelming for many students who either offer nothing or restate everything in the story. **Somebody Wanted But So** offers students a framework to help them create their summaries. Students read a story and then decide who the *Somebody* is, what that somebody *Wanted, But* what happened to keep something from happening, and *So,* finally, how everything worked out.

Somebody Wanted But So also helps students move beyond summary writing. As students choose names for the *Somebody* column, they are deciding which characters are the main characters. In the *Wanted* column, they look at events of the plot and talk about main ideas and details. With the *But* column they are examining conflict. With the *So* column they are identifying the resolution.

Somebody Wanted But So

Best Use of the Strategy

Somebody Wanted But So (MacOn et al. 1991) can be used to create and evaluate summaries and to talk about literary elements. Generally, students of all levels learn this strategy quickly and are able to use it on their own within a short period of time.

Getting the Strategy to Work

1. **To summarize** If you would like students to work on writing summaries, have them write the words *Somebody Wanted But So* on the top of their own papers. If students are reading longer works they may need to connect several statements with *and* or *then*. When using this strategy with longer works, students may write a statement after each section or include several paragraphs. Once students have completed the reading, they share all their statements, discuss differences, and, in small groups, work to develop an overall **Somebody Wanted But So** statement for the entire selection.

2. **To discuss literary elements** This strategy can also be used to focus on a specific literary element. For example, when discussing conflict, you can ask students to write **Somebody Wanted But So** statements about two characters in the same story and tell how the *But* columns differ for the two. You might also have them write two statements for the same character, one that describes an internal conflict and the other, an external conflict. When talking about point of view, you can ask students to write statements for two characters from a story and to tell how changing the character changes other aspects of the story.

Because students will create different statements for the same story, you will be able to use this strategy as an assessment tool. You can look at the statements and determine which students are still at the "and-then-this-happened" stage, which is recognizable by many statements strung together by the word *and*, and which students are able to generalize. You can quickly identify the students who do not recognize cause-and-effect relationships, which students understand main ideas and which do not, and which students can distinguish main ideas from details. You can then use students' statements to evaluate their progress.

How will students benefit from using this strategy?

- Students learn to focus on summarizing.

- Students learn to analyze characters, events, conflicts, and resolutions.

- Students write summaries from different points of view, evaluate which summaries are best, and note how changing the content in the *Somebody* column changes the other columns.

- To do this strategy, students need to identify main events, recognize cause-and-effect relationships, and decide which characters are worth discussing in depth.

Some tips for the most effective use of Somebody Wanted But So.

1. Use student's statements to evaluate their progress and to help decide what should be taught next.

2. This strategy focuses on summarizing, so it is primarily a post-reading strategy. However, it can also be used as a during-reading strategy if students are writing Somebody Wanted But So statements as they go through a book.

3. Somebody Wanted But So can be used not only as a way to teach students how to summarize, but also as a way of predicting the resolution or determining the key elements of the text (such as characters, events, or conflicts). By writing summaries from different points of view (changing the "Somebody" column), students recognize cause and effect relationships and decide which characters are worth discussing.

References:

MacOn, James M., Diane Bewell, and Maryellen Vogt. 1991. *Responses to Literature.* Newark, Del.: International Reading Association.

Strategy: Somebody Wanted But So

READING: _____

SKILL: _____

After reading the text, write **Somebody Wanted But So** statements about

_____

Somebody	Wanted	But	So

Somebody Wanted But So

Strategy: Story Impressions

Reading Skill	When can I use this strategy?		
	Prereading	**During Reading**	**Postreading**
Making Predictions	✓		
Analyzing Cause and Effect Relationships		✓	
Making Inferences		✓	
Analyzing Chronological Order			✓
Identifying Purpose			✓
Comparing and Contrasting			✓

Strategy at a Glance: Story Impressions

- The teacher chooses key words or phrases from the story the students are going to read and arranges them in a linked order.
- The class discusses the pronunciation and meaning of each word.
- Using the key words or phrases in the order they were given, students write brief summaries of what they think the story will be about.
- After reading, students compare their predictions with the actual story.

We often get impressions about texts before we read them. Sometimes those impressions are right, and sometimes they are wrong, but they help me begin to think about the text. Impressions, vague and imprecise as they are, help us predict what may happen in the text.

Some readers never form these predictions. They begin reading with no thought of what might happen; therefore, they are not using their prior experiences to help them understand the text. Predicting, or thinking ahead, is based on the ability to bring previous knowledge to a new situation. If students don't predict, they aren't using what they already know to help them understand what they are about to encounter.

The **Story Impressions** strategy helps students form an overall impression of a text. The teacher gives students 10–15 words taken from a text. Keeping these words in the order that the teacher prescribed, students write a brief paragraph that uses each word and summarizes what they think the text will be about. Creating the summary helps students focus on the text and encourages them to start thinking about the key words and concepts the teacher has chosen. Students activate prior knowledge, make predictions, and form a bridge to comprehension.

Best Use of the Strategy

When you want to encourage students to activate their prior knowledge, make predictions, recognize cause-and-effect relationships, analyze the chronological order of the events of the text, or work on vocabulary, use the **Story Impressions** strategy (McGinley and Denner 1987). The necessary preparation by the teacher is well worth the results. **Story Impressions** helps readers become engaged with a text before they begin reading. Students discuss the meaning of key words and how these words could be related, explain concepts and terms to one another, and commit their ideas to paper. They make predictions about the text based on what they know about the key words. In addition, students enjoy writing a story impression.

Getting the Strategy to Work

1. **First, choose the key words you will use.** After you read the text, choose the ten to fifteen key words, phrases, or concepts from the story. Give students enough words to form an impression, but not so many that they are able to create the entire story. If you want students to analyze the chronological order of the events in the story, identify and include expressions such as "first," "then," "afterwards," and "finally" that will enable them to sequence the events.

2. **Next, present the words and discuss their meanings.** Present the words to the students in a linked order. Go through the list with students to see whether they have any questions about the pronunciation or meaning of the words. This step helps develop students' vocabulary.

3. **Have students write and share their summaries.** After they discuss the key words and phrases, have students write a paragraph that summarizes what they think the story will be about, using all the words in their original order. It is important that students write their impressions, whether independently, with a partner, or in a large group, so that they will have something to which to refer after they have read the text. Tell students that it does not have to be a perfectly written paragraph. The point is to try to figure out how the words and phrases might be linked. Then, students share their Story Impression and discuss how they connected the key words. If you have students who are unable to see how the key words could be linked together, they may need the additional structure that the **Probable Passage** strategy on page 18 provides.

4. **Have students read the story and compare it with their Story Impressions.** After students read the story, they will want to discuss how their Story Impression differed from the actual text. Remind students that if their predictions do not match the text, that does not mean they were wrong; their predictions just differed from the text.

How will students benefit from this strategy?

- As students think about how key words connect to each other, they are predicting.
- When they create a story impression, they are forming cause-and-effect relationships and making inferences.
- As students find similarities and differences between their Story Impression and the text, they are comparing and contrasting.
- As they see how the sequencing words help them put the events in the story in a particular order, they are analyzing chronological order.

Some Tips for the Most Effective Use of Story Impressions

1. All Story Impressions need to be in writing, whether the student works independently, with a partner or in a large group. This gives students something to refer back to once they have read the text.

2. The main point of Story Impressions is to help students predict how the words could be linked so that they get an impression of the story. If students are not familiar with the key words given, go through the list and discuss their meanings as a class or in partners, so that the strategy then becomes a vocabulary strategy.

3. Make sure you give students only enough words to suggest the main idea and avoid giving away the ending of the story.

4. Story Impressions is similar to the Probable Passage strategy, but less structured. If students are unable to see how the key words could be linked together, they may benefit from the structure that Probable Passage provides.

5. Decide how much discussion students need prior to reading.

6. As students think about how key words connect to one another, they are predicting. When they create Story Impressions, they are forming cause-and- effect relationships and making inferences. As they find similarities and differences between their Story Impressions and the text, they are comparing and contrasting.

References:

McGinley, William J., and Peter R. Denner. 1987. Story Impressions: A Prereading/Writing Activity. *Journal of Reading* 31: 248-253.

Strategy: Story Impressions

READING: _____

SKILL: _____

Key Words	My Story Impression
_____ ↓ _____ ↓ _____ ↓ _____ ↓ _____ ↓ _____ ↓ _____ ↓ _____	_____ _____

Strategy: Tea Party

Reading Skill	When can I use this strategy?		
	Prereading	During Reading	Postreading
Making Predictions	✓		
Using Prior Knowledge	✓		

Strategy at a Glance: Tea Party

- The teacher selects quotations from the text, writes each quotation on a separate card, and distributes one to each student. Students share their quotations in order to form an idea about the subject of the text.

- Each student reads his or her quotation to another student, who responds by also reading a quotation.

- Small groups of students discuss the meaning of the quotations and use the passages to predict what the text will be about.

Tea Party is a strategy that helps readers become engaged with a text before they begin reading the entire selection. Students discuss the meaning of selected quotations from the story, how the passages might relate to each other, and then make predictions about the text based on the quotations.

Best Use of the Strategy

This prereading strategy gives students language to first think about and then to talk about what the text is about and concepts and ideas that may be introduced in the text. In addition, the quotations stimulate students' curiosity about the text and helps them focus on what they are reading.

Getting the Strategy to Work

1. **Select and distribute quotations from the text.** Select a text, choose 10−12 quotations from it, and prepare a list of individual quotations that can be cut into slips. (Be sure to make a master list and copies before cutting the slips. It would be helpful to number the slips or put them on different colors of paper in order to group students later for discussion.) Distribute a slip of paper to each student and ask them to share their quotations in order to form an idea about the reading selection. Have students practice reading their quotations to themselves before they share them with others. Offer to help anyone who is having problems with his or her quotation.

2. **Students read quotations to each other.** When you give the signal, students should begin to mingle; each student should walk up to a classmate and read aloud his or her quotation. The other student should respond by reading his or her quotation. Tell students that as they read their quotations to each other, they should also show one another their slips. That way, students are both seeing and listening to the quotations, thereby doubling their exposure to the text. Students should keep mingling and reading until you notice that most students have heard all the quotations and you stop the activity.

3. **Students discuss quotations and make predictions about the text.** Divide students into small groups and have them discuss their quotations and what they think they mean. Based on the quotations they have in front of them and those they heard from others, students should generalize to formulate a prediction about the subject of the reading selection.

4. **Students read the text and adjust their predictions.** As students begin to read the text, explain that active readers adjust their predictions as they learn new information or as they discover more about a character. You may want to suggest that students jot notes each time they alter their predictions as they read, indicating the information that stimulated this change. After students read the text, discuss the subject of the selection. You may wish to have students return to their groups to compare and contrast their predictions with their postreading understanding.

How do students benefit from this strategy?

- This strategy will help students as readers to begin to think about the text.

- Impressions, vague and imprecise as they are, help predict what the text is about.

- Predicting helps readers understand what they are about to encounter.

Strategy: A Tea Party

READING: _____

SKILL: _____

STRATEGIES

Strategy: Tea Party

READING: _____

SKILL: _____

Tea Party
STUDENT SHEET

I. **Directions:** Your teacher will give you a slip of paper with a quote from the reading. Write down the quote here:

_____

_____

_____

_____

II. **Directions:** Now share your quote with your classmates, and listen as they read their quotes. Based on all these quotes, what do you think the reading is about? Make your predictions here:

_____

_____

_____

_____

_____

_____

_____

You probably have some questions already. Write your questions here:

_____

_____

_____

_____

_____

Tea Party

Strategy: Text Reformulation

Reading Skill	When can I use this strategy?		
	Prereading	During Reading	Postreading
Understanding Text Structure			✓

Strategy at a Glance: Text Reformulation

- The teacher introduces **Text Reformulation** by having students reformulate a text they have read into a patterned story, such as an ABC story, or into another genre.
- The teacher models several types of reformulations.
- Either the teacher or the students choose which type of reformulation to do based on the desired learning objectives.

Sometimes by transforming a text into a different format—one that is more familiar or friendlier—students can understand it better. An example: reformulating an expository text structure to fit the narrative structure; in other words, taking what might be a difficult, even dry, expository text and retelling it as a story.

Text Reformulation, or **Story Recycling,** is a strategy in which students transform a text into another type of text.

Whether students turn expository texts into narrative, poems into newspaper articles, or short stories into patterned stories such as ABC books, reformulating texts encourages students to talk about the original texts.

Best Use of the Strategy

When students are having difficulty understanding a text, use the **Text Reformulation** (Feathers 1993), or **Story Recycling,** strategy to show them how to better understand the text by turning it into another type of text that is more familiar to them. Whether students turn expository texts into narratives, poems into newspaper articles, or short stories into patterned stories such as ABC books, reformulating texts encourages students to talk about the original texts.

Text Reformulation

Getting the Strategy to Work

1. **First, introduce the strategy.** When you introduce students to this strategy, they usually do better if you have them reformulate the text into some sort of patterned structure. There are several types of patterned structures that students can use:

   a. **Fortunately/Unfortunately structure:** "Fortunately, I set my alarm clock yesterday evening. Unfortunately, I forgot to turn the alarm on! Fortunately, my little brother woke me up. Unfortunately, he did it with his water gun."

   b. **If/Then structure:** "If the dog chases the cat, the cat will probably run up a tree. If the cat gets stuck in the tree, you will have to help get it down." Reformulating the text in this format will help them figure out cause-and-effect relationships.

   c. **Cumulative tales structure:** These are tales that build as they go, rather like the "chain" stories used in many second language classrooms. Two good examples of this are the children's rhyme "The House that Jack Built" and the song "The Twelve Days of Christmas"

   d. **ABC book structure:** "A is for _____." B is for _____."

   e. **Repetitive book structure:** Reformulating the text into a repetitive rhyme scheme, similar to "*Brown Bear, Brown Bear, What Do You See?*," a children's book by Bill Martin Jr.

2. **Model several types of reformulations.** Some students choose always to do patterned-text reformulations, such as the above; other students, though, begin to explore various types of reformulations. Students might try the following reformulations:

   - plays into short stories, comic books, letters, or interviews
   - poems into stories or letters
   - stories into plays, radio announcements, newspaper ads, or television commercials
   - plays into poems or newspaper stories
   - nonfiction (like history or science books) into stories
   - diaries or memoirs into plays, newspaper articles, or television newsmagazine scripts
   - narrative text into a biopoem (a biographical poem written according to very specific guidelines)

3. **Decide whether you or the students will choose the type of reformulation.** You can tell students what type of reformulation to use, but part of the benefit of the strategy results from their deciding exactly what type of reformulation works best. Sometimes you might want to work on cause-and-effect relationships; in that case, ask the students to reformulate using the *Fortunately/Unfortunately* or *If/then* structures. To work on characterization, suggest they reformulate the text into an interview, and to work on writing summaries, have them recycle the story into a movie preview.

4. **Provide opportunities for practice and evaluation. Text Reformulation** must be used repeatedly for students to realize its full benefits. Reformulations can be used to evaluate students' progress, but make sure that you do not penalize them for something they have omitted if you did not tell them to include it. Students will dread reading if they think they will have to rewrite the text every time. It is suggested that you introduce the strategy and model it several times with various types of reformulations.

How will students benefit from using this strategy?

- Once the students are comfortable with the strategy, they may use it to demonstrate that they can identify main ideas, sequence events, generalize, infer, analyze, and synthesize.

- In addition, reformulations encourage students to identify cause-and-effect relationships, themes, and main characters.

Some Tips for the Most Effective Use of Text Reformulation

1. Text Reformulation must be used repeatedly for students to realize its full benefits. Introduce the strategy, model it several times using different types of reformulations and then make it one way for students to demonstrate that they can identify main ideas, sequence events, generalize, infer, analyze and synthesize. More often than not, it is easy to tell whether students have used those skills just by reading their reformulations.

2. For students who 'hate' to write, offer alternatives to writing the story, for instance, recording their text reformulation on tape. You might have a group elect a scribe to do the writing, or they can take turns.

3. Keep text reformulations an option. Optional activities are generally received more favorably than required activities.

References:

Feathers, Karen. 1993. *Infotext*. Portsmouth, N. H.: Heinemann Publishers.

Strategy: Text Reformulation

READING: _____

SKILL: _____

Text

_____

_____

_____

_____

_____

_____

_____

_____

_____

_____

_____

_____

Reformulate the text

_____

_____

_____

_____

_____

_____

_____

_____

_____

_____

_____

_____

_____

Strategy: Think Aloud

Reading Skill	When can I use this strategy?		
	Prereading	During Reading	Postreading
Monitoring Reading		✓	

Strategy at a Glance: Think Aloud

- The teacher models the **Think Aloud** strategy for students, letting them tally the types of comments the teacher makes (predicting, picturing the text, comparing, commenting, identifying a problem, or fixing a problem) on the **Think Aloud** tally sheet.

- Students practice the strategy with a partner using short and easy texts before using **Think Aloud** with their assignments.

- Students regularly practice the strategy, eventually using it on their own as needed.

Many times students do what they call reading: their eyes travel over the words from left to right and from top to bottom, and they turn pages at the appropriate time. What they don't do is pay any attention to what those words mean. That is where a strategy like **Think Aloud** can help.

The **Think Aloud** strategy helps readers think about how they make meaning. As they read, they carry on a dialogue with the text. This is something that good readers do constantly as they read, although they usually do it silently. **Think Aloud** provides a structure for struggling readers to have a dialogue with a text; they learn to think about their reading and to monitor what they do and do not understand. As you monitor the comments students make while using this strategy, you will see that the student is actively engaged with the text. As they do it more often, they will learn to do it silently—and that is the goal of the strategy.

Best Use of the Strategy

Use the **Think Aloud** strategy (Davey 1983; Olshavsky 1976-77) to help readers think about how they make meaning. As students read, they pause occasionally to think aloud about predicting what happens next, commenting on the text, picturing the text, making comparisons, identifying problems they are encountering with understanding, and thinking of ways to fix the problems they identify. This oral thinking not only helps the teacher understand why or how a student is having difficulty with a text, but also encourages the student to think about the text while reading it. Students learn to think about their reading and to monitor their understanding.

Getting the Strategy to Work

1. **First, model Think Aloud.** This is truly a strategy that is not only just taught, but also shown, again and again. This strategy can be modeled using a variety of materials. Poetry, newspaper articles, sports reports, and graphs all work well as texts for **Think Aloud.** When you are modeling, read the first few paragraphs of a selection, pausing to make comments as you go. Give students a tally sheet (See the **Think Aloud Tally Sheet** on page 61). Students might disagree about whether a remark is a comparison or a comment, or whether you are visualizing or predicting. The point is for students not to guess correctly, but rather to think. This modeling process should take only about five to ten minutes of class time.

2. **After you have modeled several sample texts, have students use the strategy on a portion of text with a partner.** The partner's job is to use the tally sheet to record what type of comments the student is making.

3. **Provide ample opportunities for students to practice Think Aloud.** This is a strategy that students should internalize and use as needed, so you need to remind them frequently to use it. Students cannot go from seeing you model the strategy to using it when needed without the intermediate step of practice.

4. **Listen to students' Think Aloud and provide feedback.** Either schedule a time for students to read and think aloud to you, or have students record their Think Alouds. You may also want to have students work in pairs, taking turns commenting on the text and tallying the types of comments they hear, while you circulate and listen to students. If you hear students asking questions about the text, do not answer them while the Think Aloud is in progress. Many of these questions are often cleared up as the student continues reading. When students are finished, however, it is a good idea to ask them what questions they still have about the text. These questions can be discussed in small groups, with another reader, or with you.

How will students benefit from using this strategy?

- Students receive feedback about the types of comments they are making.

- They keep track of their comments over time and eventually begin doing what we want them to do with texts: think about them.

- When students read actively, question what they do not understand, make predictions and connections, and visualize what is going on, they have a better understanding of what they are reading.

Some Tips for the Most Effective Use of Think Aloud.

1. Many times when students first start using this strategy, they will make comments after every sentence. This may be because they are trying to get a lot of tally marks on the Think Aloud tally sheet, either because the strategy is new, or because they are avoiding reading. To help students move past this stage, give them frequent opportunities to use the strategy, so that the newness wears off. Tell students to read until they have a connection to make, a prediction to offer, or a comment to make about a problem in comprehension.

2. It is helpful to encourage students to move past one type of comment, but do not tell them what kind of Think Aloud comment to make. They need to stay focused on the text, not on the comments.

3. If a student's Think Aloud comment is a question they have about the text, do not answer it while Think Aloud is in progress. Often, confusion about what is going on in the text is cleared up as the student continues reading.

4. A Think Aloud isn't a fifty-five minute ordeal. It's a five- to ten-minute exercise that should be done approximately once a week.

5. Both Think Aloud and Say Something are metacognitive strategies that help students think about what they are reading while they are reading it. Think-Aloud, however, is done independently. The partner tallies the responses but does not participate. Say Something, on the other hand, involves interaction with a partner as students carry on a dialogue about the text.

References:

Davey, Beth. 1983. Think-Aloud: Modeling the Cognitive Processes of Reading Comprehension. *Journal of Reading* 27: 44-47.

Olshavsky, Jill Edwards. 1976-77. Reading as Problem-Solving: An Investigation of Strategies. *Reading Research Quarterly* 12: 654-674.

STRATEGIES

Name _____ Class _____ Date _____

Strategy: **Think Aloud**

READING: _____

SKILL: _____

Work with a partner to read the assigned text and make *Think Aloud* comments. One partner should read 2-3 paragraphs aloud, pausing to make comments, while the other (the listener) uses a tally mark to identify the types of comments in the *Tally* column below. Switch roles and continue to the end of the text.

Think Aloud Tally Sheet

Listener: _____

Think Aloud Comments	Tally
Identifying problems	
Fixing problems	
Predicting what happens next	
Picturing the text	
Making comparisons	
Making comments	

After your reading, answer the following questions:

1. Which types of comments did you make the most? Which type did your partner make the most?

   _____

   _____

   _____

2. How did the comments you made help you better understand the reading? Ask your partner how your comments helped him or her better understand. How did your partner's comments help you? Give a brief summary.

   _____

   _____

   _____

   _____

   _____

Think Aloud

Applying the
Reading Strategies
to
French 1 *Allez, viens!*

Chapitre 1: Petites Annonces, Pupil's Edition, pp. 36–37

SKILL: Making Generalizations
STRATEGY: Anticipation Guide

I. Before reading the "**Petites Annonces,**" read the statements below and decide whether you agree or disagree with each statement. Place an X in the appropriate space in the *Before Reading* column, and be ready to explain your decision. Then, on the lines below, predict what you think the text will be about.

Before Reading	Statement	After Reading
Agree/Disagree		**Agree/Disagree**
_____ / _____	1. Teens generally associate with those who share their interests.	_____ / _____
_____ / _____	2. Teens around the world share the same interests.	_____ / _____
_____ / _____	3. Teens have no interest in people from other countries.	_____ / _____
_____ / _____	4. Teens are only interested in friends their own age.	_____ / _____

My Prediction(s): _____

_____

_____

_____

II. After reading the text, decide if you still agree or disagree with the statements, and place an X in the appropriate space in the *After Reading* column.

III. Choose three of the Anticipation Guide Statements above. On the back of this sheet, describe how each statement relates to "**Petites Annonces.**"

_____

_____

_____

APPLYING THE STRATEGIES

Chapitre 1: Petites Annonces, Pupil's Edition, pp. 36–37

SKILL: Connecting Reading to Personal Experience
STRATEGY: Say Something

I. You and your partner should each read **"Petites Annonces"** silently. As you read, stop after each section and take turns saying something about what you just read, including any connections you can make to your own experiences. In the chart below, mark with a check the types of comments you make.

Prediction	Comment	Question	Connection

II. Think about the Say Something dialogue you had with your partner. Then, answer the following questions on the lines provided.

1. What did you and your partner talk about in the Say Something dialogue? What disagreements did you have? Give a summary.

_____

_____

_____

_____

2. Which of your comments and your partner's comments related to personal experiences?

_____

_____

_____

_____

3. How are the teenagers in the reading similar to you? In what ways are they different? What factors might account for these similarities and differences?

_____

_____

_____

_____

Chapitre 2: Sondage : les lycéens ont-ils le moral?, Pupil's Edition, pp. 64–65

SKILL: Identifying the Main Idea
STRATEGY: Read, Rate, Reread

I. Read "**Sondage : les lycéens ont-ils le moral?**" and rate your understanding of it on a scale of 1 to 10. (A score of 1 means you didn't understand it at all; a score of 10 means you understood it completely.) Record your rating in the First Rating box. Then, on the lines provided for item 1 below, write any questions you have after your first reading. Repeat this process two more times (items 2 and 3). Then, discuss any unanswered questions with a partner and rate your understanding a fourth time.

First Rating	Second Rating	Third Rating	Fourth Rating

II. Supply the following information.

1. Write down any questions you have after the first reading. Use the back of this paper to continue writing, if necessary.

_____

_____

2. Read the selection a second time and record your rating in the Second Rating box. Slow down at the parts you didn't understand the first time you read. Then, cross out any questions you can now answer. Write down any new questions you have after the second reading.

_____

_____

3. Read the selection a third time and record your rating in the Third Rating box. Cross out any questions you can now answer. Write down any new questions you have after the third reading.

_____

_____

4. After the third reading, get with a partner and see if the two of you can answer any of the questions you both still have. Cross out any questions you answer. Then, rate your understanding a fourth time and record your rating in the Fourth Rating box.

5. How did your understanding of the text change from one reading to the next? Based on your understanding of the reading, give a brief summary of the main idea of "**Sondage : les lycéens ont-ils le moral?**"

_____

_____

_____

Chapitre 2: Sondage : les lycéens ont-ils le moral?, Pupil's Edition, pp. 64–65

SKILL: Monitoring Comprehension
STRATEGY: Think-Aloud

I. Work with a partner to read "**Sondage : les lycéens ont-ils le moral?**" and make Think Aloud comments. One partner should read aloud a section of the reading, pausing to make comments, while the other partner uses a tally mark to identify the types of comments in the *Tally* column below. Then, switch roles and continue to the end of the selection.

Think Aloud Tally Sheet   Listener: _____

Think Aloud Comments	Tally
Making predictions	
Making comparisons	
Predicting what happens next	
Identifying problems	
Fixing problems	
Making a comment	

II. After your reading, answer the following questions:

1. Which types of comments did you make the most? Which type did your partner make the most?

   _____

   _____

   _____

   _____

2. How did the comments you made help you better understand the reading? Ask your partner how your comments helped him or her better understand. How did your partner's comments help you? Give a brief summary.

   _____

   _____

   _____

   _____

Chapitre 3: Univers : Tout pour la rentrée, Pupil's Edition, pp. 92–93

SKILL: Monitoring Comprehension
STRATEGY: Say Something

I. You and your partner should each read "**Univers : Tout pour la rentrée**" silently. As you read, stop after each section and take turns saying something about what you just read, including any comments you can make about monitoring your comprehension. In the chart below, mark with a check the types of comments you make.

Prediction	Comment	Question	Connection

II. Think about the Say Something dialogue you had with your partner. Then, answer the following questions on the lines provided.

1. If a third person had heard your Say Something dialogue, what would he or she have heard? Give a summary.

   _____

   _____

   _____

2. Did you answer any questions for your partner? Did your partner answer any of your questions? What were the questions? Which questions were not answered?

   _____

   _____

   _____

3. Looking at your chart above, what type of comment did you make the most? Why do you think you made this type of comment the most?

   _____

   _____

   _____

4. Think about the statements you made about monitoring your comprehension. How did the Say Something strategy help you?

   _____

   _____

APPLYING THE STRATEGIES

Chapitre 3: Univers : Tout pour la rentrée, Pupil's Edition, pp. 92–93

SKILL: Making Inferences

STRATEGY: Read, Rate, Reread

I. Read "**Univers : Tout pour la rentrée**" and rate your understanding of it on a scale of 1 to 10. (A score of 1 means you didn't understand it at all; a score of 10 means you understood it completely.) Record your rating in the First Rating box. Then, on the lines provided for item 1 below, write any questions you have after your first reading. Repeat this process two more times (items 2 and 3). Then, discuss any unanswered questions with a partner and rate your understanding a fourth time.

First Rating	Second Rating	Third Rating	Fourth Rating

II. Supply the following information.

A. Write down any questions you have after the first reading. Use the back of this paper to continue writing, if necessary.

_____

_____

_____

B. Read the selection a second time and record your rating in the Second Rating box. Slow down at the parts you didn't understand the first time you read. Then, cross out any questions you can now answer. Write down any new questions you have after the second reading.

_____

_____

C. Read the selection a third time and record your rating in the Third Rating box. Cross out any questions you can now answer. Write down any new questions you have after the third reading.

_____

_____

D. After the third reading, get with a partner and see if the two of you can answer any of the questions you both still have. Cross out any questions you answer. Then, rate your understanding a fourth time and record your rating in the Fourth Rating box.

E. How did your understanding of the text change from one reading to the next. Using the text and accompanying photos, what inferences could you make that helped you better understand the reading? Give a brief summary.

_____

_____

_____

APPLYING THE STRATEGIES

Chapitre 4: Allez, c'est à vous de choisir!, Pupil's Edition, pp. 126–127

SKILL: Making Predictions
STRATEGY: Tea Party

I. Mingle among several of your classmates. For each classmate you meet, you should read the quotation on the card you have been given, and he or she should read the quotation on his or her card. Then, in small groups discuss what you think **"Allez, c'est à vous de choisir!"** will be about. Briefly summarize your predictions below.

_____

_____

_____

_____

II. Now, either alone or in your group, read **"Allez, c'est à vous de choisir!"** and answer the questions that follow.

1. Briefly summarize the reading.

_____

_____

_____

_____

2. How do your predictions of the contents of the reading differ from its actual contents? In what ways were your predictions accurate?

_____

_____

_____

_____

APPLYING THE STRATEGIES

SKILL: Making Predictions
STRATEGY: Tea Party

Il n'y a pas d'âge pour commencer.

On découvre à la fois les joies et les doutes de l'improvisation et les grands auteurs.

Avec quelques copains et un ballon, on peut s'amuser presque partout.

Peu de garçons s'inscrivent au cours de danse et c'est bien dommage.

Des matches sont organisés par les clubs.

Il existe une formule de location de kart, avec cours adaptés dès l'âge de douze ans.

Vous devez avoir votre instrument.

Chapitre 4: Allez, c'est à vous de choisir!, Pupil's Edition, pp. 126–127

SKILL: Monitoring Comprehension
STRATEGY: Think Aloud

I. Work with a partner to read "**Allez, c'est à vous de choisir!**" and make Think Aloud comments. One partner should read aloud a section of the reading, pausing to make comments, while the other partner uses a tally mark to identify the types of comments in the *Tally* column below. Then, switch roles and continue to the end of the selection.

Think Aloud Tally Sheet   Listener: _____

Think Aloud Comments	Tally
Making predictions	
Making comparisons	
Identifying problems	
Fixing problems	
Picturing the text	
Making a comment	

II. Answer the following questions.

1. Which types of comments did you make the most? Which type did your partner make the most?

   _____

   _____

2. How did the comments you made help you better understand the reading? Ask your partner how your comments helped him or her better understand. How did your partner's comments help you? Give a brief summary.

   _____

   _____

   _____

   _____

Chapitre 5: Des menus de cafés, Pupil's Edition, pp. 158–159

SKILL: Making Inferences
STRATEGY: Read, Rate, Reread

I. Read **"Café des Lauriers"** and **"Fontaine Elysée"** and rate your understanding on a scale of 1 to 10. (A score of 1 means you didn't understand it at all; a score of 10 means you understood it completely.) Record your rating in the First Rating box. Then, on the lines provided for item 1 below, write any questions you have after your first reading. Repeat this process two more times (items 2 and 3). Then, discuss any unanswered questions with a partner and rate your understanding a fourth time.

First Rating	Second Rating	Third Rating	Fourth Rating

II. Supply the following information.

1. Write down any questions you have after the first reading. Use the back of this paper to continue writing, if necessary.

_____

_____

_____

2. Read the selection a second time and record your rating in the Second Rating box. Slow down at the parts you didn't understand the first time you read. Then, cross out any questions you can now answer. Write down any new questions you have after the second reading.

_____

_____

3. Read the selection a third time and record your rating in the Third Rating box. Cross out any questions you can now answer. Write down any new questions you have after the third reading.

_____

_____

4. After the third reading, get with a partner and see if the two of you can answer any of the questions you both still have. Cross out any questions you answer. Then, rate your understanding a fourth time and record your rating in the Fourth Rating box.

5. How did your understanding of the text change from one reading to the next. Using the text and accompanying photos, what inferences could you make that helped you better understand the reading? Give a brief summary.

_____

_____

_____

Chapitre 5: Des menus de cafés, Pupil's Edition, pp. 158–159

SKILL: Monitoring Comprehension
STRATEGY: Say Something

I. You and your partner should each read **"Café des Lauriers"** and **"Fontaine Elysée"** silently. Before you begin to read, divide the reading into short sections. As you read, stop after each section and take turns saying something about what you just read, including any comments you can make about monitoring your comprehension. In the chart below, mark with a check the types of comments you make.

Prediction	Comment	Question	Connection

II. Think about the Say Something dialogue you had with your partner. Then, answer the following questions on the lines provided.

1. If a third person had heard your Say Something dialogue, what would he or she have heard? Give a summary.

   _____

   _____

2. Did you answer any questions for your partner? Did your partner answer any of your questions? What were the questions? Which questions were not answered?

   _____

   _____

3. Looking at your chart above, what type of comment did you make the most? Why do you think you made this type of comment the most?

   _____

   _____

4. Think about the statements you made about monitoring your comprehension. How did the Say Something strategy help you?

   _____

   _____

5. How did the French words you already know and your knowledge of cognates help your comprehension of this reading?

   _____

   _____

Chapitre 6: Parcs d'attractions, Pupil's Edition, pp. 188–189

SKILL: Monitoring Comprehension
STRATEGY: Think Aloud

I. Work with a partner to read **"Le Pays France Miniature," "Parc Astérix,"** and **"Parc Zoologique de Paris"** and make Think Aloud comments. One partner should read aloud a section of the reading, pausing to make comments, while the other partner uses a tally mark to identify the types of comments in the *Tally* column below. Then, switch roles and continue to the end of the selection.

Think Aloud Tally Sheet   Listener: _____

Think Aloud Comments	Tally
Making predictions	
Making comparisons	
Identifying problems	
Recognizing cognates	
Fixing problems	
Making a comment	

II. Answer the following questions.

1. Which types of comments did you make the most? Which type did your partner make the most?

   _____

   _____

2. How did the comments you made help you better understand the reading? Ask your partner how your comments helped him or her better understand. How did your partner's comments help you? Give a brief summary.

   _____

   _____

3. How many comments did you make about recognizing cognates? How valuable are cognates when trying to understand a reading in a different language? Explain.

   _____

   _____

APPLYING THE STRATEGIES

Chapitre 6: Parcs d'attractions, Pupil's Edition, pp. 188–189

SKILL: Making Predictions
STRATEGY: Tea Party

I. Mingle among several of your classmates. For each classmate you meet, you should read the quotation on the card you have been given, and he or she should read the quotation on his or her card. Then, in small groups discuss what you think **"Le Pays France Miniature," "Parc Astérix,"** and **"Parc Zoologique de Paris"** will be about. Briefly summarize your predictions below.

_____

_____

_____

_____

_____

_____

II. Now, either alone or in your group, read **"Le Pays France Miniature," "Parc Astérix,"** and **"Parc Zoologique de Paris"** and answer the questions that follow.

1. Briefly summarize the reading.

_____

_____

_____

_____

2. How do your predictions of the contents of the reading differ from its actual contents? In what ways were your predictions accurate?

_____

_____

_____

3. What made the use of the Tea Party strategy more challenging for this reading than it might have been for a short story or a newspaper article?

_____

_____

_____

APPLYING THE STRATEGIES

Chapitre 6: Parcs d'attractions, Pupil's Edition, pp. 188–189

SKILL: Making Predictions
STRATEGY: Tea Party

Le Pays FRANCE MINIATURE, c'est la France comme vous ne l'avez jamais vue.

Pour un un voyage mémorable en Gaule, au pays du bon vivre et de l'histoire.

Ouverture : 15 mars au 15 novembre

Prix par personne : 52 euros

Ouvert tous les jours.

Sur une immense carte en relief, sont regroupées les plus belles richesses de notre patrimoine.

Astérix et tous ses amis vous y attendent.

Chapitre 7: En Direct des Refuges, Pupil's Edition, pp. 216–217

SKILL: Understanding Text Structure
STRATEGY: Text Reformulation

I. First, read "**En Direct des Refuges.**" Then, you will reformulate each section of the reading into a Fortunately (**Heureusement**)/Unfortunately (**Malheureusement**) structure. For example, you might begin to reformulate the section about **Camel** like this:

> Heureusement Camel est un chien sympathique. Malheureusement, il est au refuge parce qu'il n'a pas de maître. Heureusement, on peut adopter Camel. Malheureusement, il est grand et il a besoin d'un grand espace.

II. Write your reformulations in the spaces provided below.

Camel

_____
_____
_____

Dady

_____
_____
_____

Mayo

_____
_____
_____

Poupette

_____
_____
_____
_____

Jupiter

_____
_____
_____
_____

Flora

_____
_____

Chapitre 7: En Direct des Refuges, Pupil's Edition, pp. 216–217

SKILL: Understanding Text Structure
STRATEGY: Logographic Cues

I. "En Direct des Refuges" is a collection of articles from a French magazine that deal with pets that are up for adoption. To help you better understand the articles and to understand the structure of the articles, create logographic cues that relate to each of the following significant characteristics of the articles. Then, as you read the articles, place your logographic cues next to the portions of the article that deal with each specific characteristic.

1. **Description of the Pet**

   A. **Physical Characteristics**

   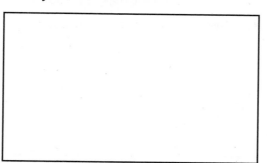

   B. **Personality Characterisitics**

   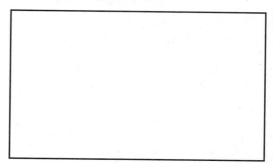

2. **Reason Pet is in the Shelter**

   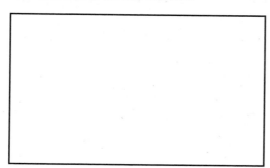

3. **Where the Pet Can Be Adopted**

   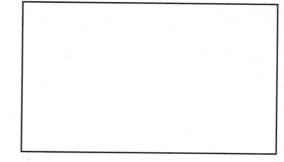

APPLYING THE STRATEGIES

Chapitre 8: La Cuisine Africaine, Pupil's Edition, pp. 250–251

SKILL: Making Predictions
STRATEGY: Tea Party

I. Mingle among several of your classmates. For each classmate you meet, you should read the quotation on the card you have been given, and your classmate should read the quotation on his or her card. Then, in small groups discuss what you think **"La Cuisine Africaine"** will be about. Briefly summarize your predictions below.

_____

_____

_____

II. Now, either alone or in your group, read **"La Cuisine Africaine"** and answer the questions that follow.

1. Briefly summarize the reading.

_____

_____

_____

_____

2. How do your predictions of the contents of the reading differ from its actual contents? In what ways were your predictions accurate?

_____

_____

_____

_____

SKILL: Making Predictions
STRATEGY: Tea Party

Mélanger la noix de coco râpée.

Etaler la pâte sur 1/2 cm.

Découper (la pâte) en croissants.

Epucher les concombres.

Egréner le maïs.

Retirer le chapeau des brioches.

Arroser la salade de jus de lime.

Chapitre 8: La Cuisine Africaine, Pupil's Edition, pp. 250–251

SKILL: Monitoring Comprehension
STRATEGY: Read, Rate, Reread

APPLYING THE STRATEGIES

I. Read "**La Cuisine Africaine**" and rate your understanding on a scale of 1 to 10. (A score of 1 means you didn't understand it at all; a score of 10 means you understood it completely.) Record your rating in the First Rating box. Then, on the lines provided for item 1 below, write any questions you have after your first reading. Repeat this process two more times (items 2 and 3). Then, discuss any unanswered questions with a partner and rate your understanding a fourth time.

First Rating	Second Rating	Third Rating	Fourth Rating

II. Supply the following information.

1. Write down any questions you have after the first reading. Use the back of this paper to continue writing, if necessary.

    _____

    _____

2. Read the selection a second time and record your rating in the Second Rating box. Slow down at the parts you didn't understand the first time you read. Then, cross out any questions you can now answer. Write down any new questions you have after the second reading.

    _____

    _____

3. Read the selection a third time and record your rating in the Third Rating box. Cross out any questions you can now answer. Write down any new questions you have after the third reading.

    _____

    _____

4. After the third reading, get with a partner and see if the two of you can answer any of the questions you both still have. Cross out any questions you answer. Then, rate your understanding a fourth time and record your rating in the Fourth Rating box.

5. How did your understanding of the text change from one reading to the next? Give a brief summary.

    _____

    _____

Chapitre 9: Je passe ma vie au téléphone, Pupil's Edition, pp. 282–283

SKILL: Making Inferences

STRATEGY: It Says ... I Say

I. After you have read "**Je passe ma vie au téléphone,**" answer the questions in the following chart. You may have several comments under the *It Says* and *I Say* columns for each question, but you will only have one answer under the *And So* column for each question. The answer you write in the *And So* column is your inference. Continue your answers on another sheet of paper if necessary.

Question	It Says ... + (What the text says)	I Say ... = (My thoughts)	And So ... (My inference)
Emmanuelle 1. Where did Emmanuelle learn to talk so long on the phone?			
Emmanuelle 2. How does Emmanuelle feel now about using the phone?			
Géraldine 3. What is Géraldine's relationship with the telephone?			
Pour dire bonjour, pour un rien... 4. Is Véronique or Aurélie the parent in this passage? How can you tell?			

APPLYING THE STRATEGIES

Reading Strategies and Skills Handbook **85**

Chapitre 9: Je passe ma vie au téléphone, Pupil's Edition, pp. 282–283

SKILL: Determining the Main Idea
STRATEGY: Save the Last Word for Me

I. After you have read "**Je passe ma vie au téléphone**," choose your favorite passage and copy it on the lines provided.

_____

_____

_____

_____

_____

_____

_____

_____

II. Directions: On the lines provided, answer the following questions.

1. Why did you choose this passage?

_____

_____

_____

2. How does this passage reveal important ideas in "**Je passe ma vie au téléphone**"?

_____

_____

_____

_____

III. Directions: Discuss you favorite passage either with a group or with a partner, discussing your answers to the questions above. Then answer the following question.

How did your choice of a favorite passage differ from the choice(s) of your group or partner? Give a brief summary.

_____

_____

_____

_____

APPLYING THE STRATEGIES

Chapitre 10: La Mode au Lycée, Pupil's Edition, pp. 312–313

SKILL: Making Inferences

STRATEGY: It Says ... I Say

I. After you have read "**La Mode au Lycée,**" answer the questions in the following chart. You may have several comments under the *It Says* and *I Say* columns for each question, but you will only have one answer under the *And So* column for each question. The answer you write in the *And So* column is your inference. Continue your answers on another sheet of paper if necessary.

Question	It Says ... + (What the text says)	I Say ... = (My thoughts)	And So ... (My inference)
Mélanie How does Mélanie feel about today's fashion?			
Christophe How fashion-conscious is Christophe?			
Serge Would Serge feel comfortable wearing clothes by Ralph Lauren or Tommy Hilfiger?			
Emmanuelle Would Emmanuelle be likely to dress in the most popular fashions?			

APPLYING THE STRATEGIES

Chapitre 10: La Mode au Lycée, Pupil's Edition, pp. 312–313

SKILL: Determining the Main Idea
STRATEGY: Most Important Word

I. After you have read **"La Mode au Lycée,"** review the reading and choose three words that you think are important. In the chart below, write each word in the left-hand column. In the right-hand column, explain why you think each word may be the most important. Use examples from the text to support each word choice.

Important Words	Why This Word Is Important in the Reading
1.	
2.	
3.	

II. Look at the chart above and the reasons for each word choice. Then, complete the following items on the lines provided.

A. After thinking about my word choices in Part I, I think the most important word in this reading is:

_____

B. How does this word relate to the reading?

_____

C. Using your most important word, write a sentence that states the main idea of the reading.

_____

_____

III. Directions: In a small group, share and discuss the most important words chosen by the members of the group. What do you think about the words chosen by the other group members? Do you agree or disagree with their reasons for choosing their words? After you have finished your discussion, complete the following items on the lines provided.

1. After my group's discussion, I think _____ is the most important word.

2. I changed/didn't change my mind because _____

_____

3. Now I think/still think that the main idea of the reading is _____

_____

Chapitre 11: Un guide touristique, Pupil's Edition, pp. 340–341

SKILL: Monitoring Comprehension
STRATEGY: Say Something

I. You and your partner should each read the selections from "**Un guide touristique**" silently. As you read, stop after each section and take turns saying something about what you just read, including any comments you can make about monitoring your comprehension. In the chart below, mark with a check the types of comments you make.

Prediction	Comment	Question	Connection

II. Think about the Say Something dialogue you had with your partner. Then, answer the following questions on the lines provided.

1. If a third person had heard your Say Something dialogue, what would he or she have heard? Give a summary.

_____

_____

2. Did you answer any questions for your partner? Did your partner answer any of your questions? What were the questions? Which questions were not answered?

_____

_____

3. Looking at your chart above, what type of comment did you make the most? Why do you think you made this type of comment the most?

_____

_____

4. Think about the statements you made about monitoring your comprehension. How did the Say Something strategy help you?

_____

_____

_____

Chapitre 11: Un guide touristique, Pupil's Edition, pp. 340–341

SKILL: Monitoring Comprehension
STRATEGY: Think Aloud

I. Work with a partner to read the selections from **"Un guide touristique"** and make Think Aloud comments. One partner should read aloud a section of the reading, pausing to make comments, while the other partner uses a tally mark to identify the types of comments in the *Tally* column below. Then, switch roles and continue to the end of the selection.

Think Aloud Tally Sheet   Listener: _____

Think Aloud Comments	Tally
Making predictions	
Making comparisons	
Identifying problems	
Fixing problems	
Recognizing cognates	
Making a comment	

II. Answer the following questions.

1. Which types of comments did you make the most? Which type did your partner make the most?

   _____

   _____

2. How did the comments you made help you better understand the reading? Ask your partner how your comments helped him or her better understand. How did your partner's comments help you? Give a brief summary.

   _____

   _____

   _____

   _____

Chapitre 12: Cheval de bois, Pupil's Edition, pp. 374–375

SKILL: Making Predictions
STRATEGY: Story Impressions

I. Before reading the selection entitled "**Cheval de bois,**" study the key words below from the selection and decide how you think they are related. Then, use the words in the order they are given to write a Story Impression that tells what you think the selection will be about. Before you begin, find any sequence words in the list. These words will help you arrange your Story Impression in chronological order.

Key Words	My Story Impression
la ville de Saint-Pierre	_____
↓	_____
le manège	_____
↓	_____
une fête patronale	_____
↓	_____
six chevaux de bois	_____
↓	_____
le soir	_____
↓	_____
le cheval bleu	_____
↓	_____
un rêve	_____
↓	_____
visiter le monde	_____
↓	_____
le matin	_____
↓	_____
un enfant	_____
↓	_____
une bête dans le cheval	_____
↓	_____
le sage Congo	_____
↓	_____
un grand feu	_____
↓	_____
la nuit	_____
↓	_____
dépose	_____
↓	_____
un immense oiseau bleu	_____

APPLYING THE STRATEGIES

II. After reading "**Cheval de bois,**" review your Story Impression. How close was your prediction to the events in the actual story? On the back of this sheet, explain how your Story Impression is similar to and/or different from the actual story.

Chapitre 12: Cheval de bois, Pupil's Edition, pp. 374–375

SKILL: Making Predictions
STRATEGY: Probable Passage

I. Study the following words and phrases and arrange them into the categories below. Then, referring to your categorized list when necessary, complete the probable passage. When you have finished the Probable Passage, read the selection **"Cheval de bois"** and complete Part 2.

Words and Phrases to sort:

la ville de Saint-Pierre	visiter	joue	les jeunes gens
le cheval de bois bleu	s'envole	dépose	un enfant
le sage Congo	installent	un immense oiseau bleu	le rêve
construit	chevaux de bois	a peur	

Categories for Sorting Words and Phrases	
Setting	
Characters	
Actions	

Probable Passage:

(1) _____ a une grande fête patronale. Les gens (2) _____

un manège avec six (3) _____. La famille Quinquina

(4) _____ de la musique et (5) _____ poussent le manège.

Le soir, (6) _____ a un rêve. Il veut (7) _____ le monde.

Au matin, (8) _____ qui monte le cheval sent son rêve et il

(9) _____. Les gens de la ville appellent (10) _____. Il

parle au cheval bleu et il (11) _____ un grand feu. Le soir, Congo (12)

_____ le cheval de bois dans le feu. (13) _____ du cheval

s'élève du feu comme (14) _____ et (15) _____ vers

l'horizon.

II. Directions: Complete the following statement on the lines provided.

My Probable Passage differed from the selection **"Cheval de bois"** in the following ways:

_____

_____

References

Blau, Sheridan. 1992. The Writing Process and the Teacher of Literature. Keynote address given at the annual meeting of the Greater Dallas Council of Teachers of English, 15 February, 1992, Fort Worth, Texas.

Bleich, David. 1975. *Readings and Feelings: An Introduction to Subjective Criticism.* Urbana, Illinois: National Council of Teachers of English.

Davey, Beth. 1983. Think-Aloud: Modeling the Cognitive Processes of Reading Comprehension. *Journal of Reading* 27: 44-47.

Feathers, Karen. 1993. *Infotext.* Portsmouth, N. H.: Heinemann Publishers.

Harste, Jerome C. and Carolyn L. Burke, 1988. *Creating Classrooms for Authors.* Portsmouth, N.H. Heinemann Publishers.

Harste, Jerome C., Kathy Gnagey Short, and Carolyn L. Burke. 1988. *Creating Classrooms for Authors: The Reading-Writing Connection.* Portsmouth, N.H.: Heinemann Publishers.

Olshavsky, Jill Edwards. 1976-77. Reading as Problem-Solving: An Investigation of Strategies. *Reading Research Quarterly* 12: 654-674.

Short, Kathy Gnagey, Jerome C. Harste, and Carolyn L. Burke. 1996. *Creating Classrooms for Authors and Inquirers.* 2nd ed. Portsmouth, N. H.: Heinemann Publishers.

Tierney, Robert J., John E. Readance, and Ernest K. Dishner. 1995. *Reading Strategies and Practices: A Compendium.* 4th ed. Needham Heights, Mass.: Allyn and Bacon.

Wood, Karen D. 1984. Probable Passages: A Writing Strategy. *The Reading Teacher* 37: 496-499.

MacOn, James M., Diane Bewell, and Maryellen Vogt. 1991. *Responses to Literature.* Newark, Del.: International Reading Association.

McGinley, William J., and Peter R. Denner. 1987. Story Impressions: A Prereading/Writing Activity. *Journal of Reading* 31: 248-253.